LOVING THE CHURCH

CHRISTOPH SCHÖNBORN

Loving the Church

Spiritual Exercises Preached in the Presence of Pope John Paul II

TRANSLATED BY JOHN SAWARD

SAN FRANCISCO   IGNATIUS PRESS

Spiritual Exercises preached from
February 25, 1996, to February 30, 1996

Original Italian edition: *Amare la Chiesa. Esercizi Spiritual
predicati al Papa Giovanni Paolo II*
© 1997 Edizioni San Paolo, s.r.l., Cimisello Balsamo, Milan

Cover art: *Sermon on the Mount* (detail)
Fra Angelico
From the Museo San Marco, Florence, Italy
Scala/Art Resource, N.Y.

Cover design by Roxanne Mei Lum

To the Priests of the Archdiocese of Vienna
as a sign of gratitude and encouragement

CONTENTS

7

TRANSLATOR'S NOTE

Scriptural quotations have in most cases been taken from the Revised Standard Version. The translations of the documents of the Second Vatican Council are either the version given in the *Catechism of the Catholic Church* or my own translations from the Latin text. Translations of prayers from the *Missale romanum* (1970) are my own work and not the ICEL version currently in use.

ABBREVIATIONS

AG   Vatican Council II, Decree on the Church's Missionary Activity *Ad gentes divinitus* (December 7, 1965)

CCC   *Catechism of the Catholic Church*

CT   John Paul II, apostolic exhortation *Catechesi tradendae* (October 16, 1979)

DEV   John Paul II, encyclical *Dominum et vivificantem* (May 18, 1986)

FD   John Paul II, apostolic constitution *Fidei depositum* (October 11, 1992)

GS   Vatican Council II, Pastoral Constitution on the Church in the Modern World *Gaudium et spes* (December 7, 1965)

LG   Vatican Council II, Dogmatic Constitution on the Church *Lumen Gentium* (November 21, 1964)

MD   John Paul II, apostolic letter *Mulieris dignitatem* (August 1, 1988)

PDV   John Paul II, apostolic exhortation *Pastores dabo vobis* (March 25, 1992)

SC   Vatican Council II, Constitution on the Sacred Liturgy *Sacrosanctum concilium* (December 4, 1963)

STh   Saint Thomas Aquinas, *Summa theologiae*

TMA   John Paul II, apostolic letter *Tertio millennio adveniente* (November 10, 1994)

Emphasis has been added to many of the quotations from Scripture, Church documents, and other sources in accordance with the original German text.

INTRODUCTION

Holy Father, my dear brothers in the episcopate and priesthood,

> God [is] infinitely perfect and blessed in himself (CCC 1).

With these words begins the *Catechism of the Catholic Church*, and with these same words we begin these days of spiritual exercises. They are meant to show the "place" to which our Lord is inviting us during these days, the place where we find his "rest" (cf. Heb 4:11). "Rabbi, where are you staying?" That was the question of the first disciples on that unforgettable day when they met HIM for the first time, when he turned and saw them and said: "What do you seek?" (Jn 1:38). " 'Rabbi, where are you staying?' He said to them, 'Come and see.' They came and saw where he was staying; and they stayed with him that day, for it was about the tenth hour" (Jn 1:38–39). That first meeting lives on in the mind of the "disciple whom Jesus loved". Even in old age, he remembers, "It was about the tenth hour", about four in the afternoon. From this first hour, a community began, a communion of life with him began, *the Church* began. For what is the Church if not living "*communion with Jesus Christ*" (as *Catechesi tradendae* says)?[1] The Church began when John

---

[1] John Paul II, apostolic exhortation *Catechesi tradendae* (October 16, 1979), no. 5 (abbreviated hereafter as CT); CCC 426.

the Baptist pointed Jesus out to "two of his disciples", who were standing with him: "And he looked at Jesus as he walked, and said, 'Behold, the Lamb of God!'" (Jn 1:35–36). This meeting with him, and thus the beginning of that living communion with him that we call the Church, had a long *preparation*. It required many centuries of "God and man becoming accustomed to one another", as Saint Irenaeus puts it (CCC 53), before *the hour* was ripe. Only then could men be taken to the place where the Lord dwells, the place to which, from the beginning, he has invited mankind.

As always in the Gospel of John, visible and invisible, heavenly and earthly, are intertwined: "Where are you staying?" That is the simple question of two rather gauche fellows who do not know how to start a conversation. And yet the whole quest of mankind resounds through their question, the question about the One with whom men once enjoyed an intimacy that now they have lost: "Rabbi, where are you staying?" And the longing behind this question is already a call to him who, from the first hour, has been calling men: "Adam, where are you?" (Gen 3:9).

And so, as the Apostle looks back in his old age, that first hour seems heavy with mystery, the *Mystery of the Beginning*—not just of the beginning in the chronological sense, the moment in time of that first meeting, but also the *source* of the meeting *in the beginning* in which God created heaven and earth (Gen 1:1), and even more deeply in that beginning in which the Word was, in which the Word was with God and was God and is God and remains God forever (cf. Jn 1:1).

For the aged Apostle, the moment of the first meeting

is bathed in the light of that *beginning*, that source, which is God's most proper mystery. Here began the path to intimate friendship with Jesus, a path on which John and the others who soon came after were led by Jesus himself into the *innermost place* where *he* dwells. In the bright light of Easter faith, John says of this place: "No one has ever seen God. The only begotten Son, who is in the bosom of the Father, he has made him known" (Jn 1:18). It is into this "place of his rest", the bosom of the Father, that Jesus will usher John and the others. It is from this place that Jesus comes, and of this place *he alone* brings knowledge (Jn 1:18). And the knowledge that the Only-begotten, the Son, brings from the heart of the Father is this: "Father, . . . this is eternal life, that they know thee, the only true God, and Jesus Christ whom thou hast sent" (Jn 17:3). There, in the heart of the Father, rests the Son, and from there comes the decision to create the world, the plan of the community that is called and is the Church.

All this is still hidden at that first moment of meeting. What did Jesus say to them at that time, when they "stayed with him that day" (Jn 1:39)? Strangely, John is silent about it, even though he, like no other evangelist, reports the most intimate words of Jesus to his disciples (Jn 13–17). The first meeting remains as a mystery in his heart. And yet it is as if all that follows is already hidden within the mystery of this hour. We learn how decisive these hours with Jesus were from what happens the next day. Andrew brings Simon to Jesus: "We have found the Messiah" (Jn 1:41). And the day after that, Nathanael says to Jesus, "Rabbi, you are the Son of God! You are the King of Israel!" (Jn 1:49).

At the beginning of this retreat, we are being invited,

with John and like John, to look back at the first moment when *we* met our Lord, when he addressed the question to *us*, "What is it you seek?" For every person, the call of Christ has a unique, unmistakable character—today just as at the beginning of the Church. And just as John kept the memory of the first meeting as his own secret, so we, too, cannot express in words what happened so deep within ourselves when we were called, even when we can speak about its outward circumstances. Still, in a retreat, we can and should go back, in a personal way, to that beginning, whatever it was like, so that we can find *him* anew and see and contemplate "where he lives" (Jn 1:39) and *stay* there with him. Then we can once more do what Andrew did for his brother Simon: "He brought him to Jesus" (Jn 1:42). What more beautiful gift can spiritual exercises give us than the ability to say: "We have found Christ" (Jn 1:41) and to confess with Nathanael: "Rabbi, you are the Son of God! You are the King of Israel" (Jn 1:49)? May the personal grace of these spiritual exercises be this: the joy, ever ancient and ever new, the never-aging joy, of being able to say, "We have found Christ!"

And yet the goal and quest of these spiritual exercises should not be just a *personal* meeting with our Lord. Andrew says to his brother Simon, "*We* have found Christ." From the beginning, there is this "we"! They followed Jesus in twos. *Together* they stayed with him; *together* they say whom they have found; *together* will he later send them out. The first meeting with Jesus was like the *moment of the Church's birth*. For what will soon be two thousand years, she has been walking her pilgrim's path, and now she is getting ready to celebrate the jubilee, the commemoration, of her own birth in the coming of the Messiah, in the birth of the Son of God. Everything in the Church is at once *totally personal* and *totally common*, a personal vocation and a common vocation, and so, during this retreat, our eyes should be not only on our own vocation but on the mission of the Church. Our deeply personal call from Christ is also an integration into the "we" of the Church. During these days we shall contemplate her "place", her "birth", her path, and her goal. So, alongside a new joy in our personal vocation, may the Lord also renew in us a love for the Church, his Bride. To serve is the vocation and task of us all. Who is she in the deepest wellsprings of her being: that is to be the theme of our meditations. But if we are to love the Church more, we must see her with the eyes of Jesus, who "loved the Church and gave himself up for her" (Eph 5:25), just as he "loved me and gave himself for *me*" (Gal 2:20).

The plan of our meditations will follow a text from the Second Vatican Council's Constitution on the Church. In its first chapter, on "The Mystery of the Church", *Lumen Gentium* presents the Church as "a people brought into unity from the unity of the Father, the Son, and the Holy Spirit".[2] The growth and unfolding of the Church takes place in five great stages. These do not, of course, simply supersede one another. Rather, they take place alongside and inside each other, and as such they constitute the entire reality of the Church. The Council says of the Church that:

---

[2] Dogmatic Constitution on the Church, *Lumen Gentium* (November 21, 1964) no. 4 (abbreviated hereafter as LG); CCC 810.

1. "[She was] already present in figure at the beginning of the world."

2. "[She] was prepared in marvellous fashion in the history of the people of Israel and the Old Covenant."

3. "[She was] established in this last age of the world."

4. "[She was] made manifest in the outpouring of the Holy Spirit."

5. "[She] will be brought to glorious completion at the end of time."[3]

Each of the five days of our retreat will be devoted to one of these stages. Constant reference will be made to the *Catechism of the Catholic Church*. In the words of the Holy Father, the Catechism is meant to express "the symphony of the faith",[4] and so in the meditations we shall try to "hear all the notes together" and see all the parts as a whole: "In reading the *Catechism of the Catholic Church*, we can perceive the wonderful unity of the mystery of God, his saving will, as well as the central place of Jesus Christ, the only-begotten Son of God" (FD 2).

It is significant that, in *Pastores dabo vobis*,[5] the Holy Father recommends the study of the Catechism to seminarians, so that they can get a global view of the doctrine of the faith. May the Catechism also help us in this retreat to grow stronger in faith, as men receptive and

[3] LG 2; CCC 759.
[4] Apostolic constitution *Fidei depositum* (October 11, 1992), no. 1 (abbreviated hereafter as FD).
[5] John Paul II, apostolic exhortation *Pastores dabo vobis* (March 25, 1992), no. 62 (abbreviated hereafter as PDV).

ready to listen to our Mother, the Church, whose children we are privileged to remain, even as pastors. The Catechism puts it this way: "As a mother who teaches her children to speak and so to understand and communicate, the Church our Mother teaches us the language of faith in order to introduce us to the understanding and the life of faith" (CCC 171).

But, to conclude, let us return to that first sentence of our introduction, the first sentence of the Catechism: "God is infinitely perfect and blessed in himself." The first word of the Catechism is *God*. I am also tempted to say that the first statement of the Catechism is a *cry of jubilation*: "God is infinitely perfect and blessed in himself." *Adoration* resounds through this first foundational confession: *God* is infinitely worthy of worship. Praising him requires no justification. He is infinitely worthy of praise. And yet he does not need our praise. It can add nothing to him. He lacks nothing: God is *infinitely happy* in himself. For contemplating him, for praising him, for worshipping him, he is reason enough himself.

Father Réginald Garrigou-Lagrange, O.P., used to give a public lecture every Saturday in the *aula magna* of the Angelicum in Rome. These lectures were attended by large numbers of people, including lay people from the city. One Saturday Father Garrigou-Lagrange was just beginning his lecture. The first word was "God". He said the word—and then fell silent. After a while he began again, but, having said the word "God", he was unable to utter another syllable. Everyone waited, tense and silent. Then he closed his book, stood up, and went away . . . The eyewitness who reported this to me—he is still alive

—concluded the story with this comment: "It was the most impressive theology lecture I have ever heard."

God is infinitely happy and perfect in himself, and for that reason, *and only for that reason*, all that he does is done "out of pure goodness", out of love. Nothing forces him. He does not need us to fulfill himself. God alone is (CCC 212). We shall never exhaust what he is, never comprehend who he is: "Si comprehenderis, non est Deus."[6] And yet we shall participate in his happiness. For that we were created: "God . . . in a plan of sheer goodness freely created man to make him share in his own blessed life." What now follows in this first paragraph of the Catechism is a kind of summary of the theme of these spiritual exercises: "For this reason, at every time and in every place, God draws close to man. He calls man to seek him, to know him, to love him with all his strength. He calls together all men, scattered and divided by sin, into the unity of his family, the Church. To accomplish this, when the fullness of time had come, God sent his Son as Redeemer and Savior. In his Son and through him, he invites men to become, in the Holy Spirit, his adopted children and thus heirs of his blessed life" (CCC 1).

O lux beata Trinitas	O Trinity of blessèd light,
et principalis Unitas	O Unity of princely might,
iam sol recedit igneus;	The fiery sun now goes his way;
infunde lumen cordibus.	Shed thou within our hearts thy ray.

---

[6] St. Augustine, *Sermo* 52, 6, 16; CCC 230.

Thus we pray in the hymn for Vespers on Sundays in Ordinary Time. On the evening of this day, let us ask the triune God to pour into our hearts during this retreat the light that *he himself is*: "O lux, beata Trinitas!"

"THE CHURCH WAS ALREADY PRESENT IN FIGURE AT THE BEGINNING OF THE WORLD"

First Meditation
The Church Is the Goal of All Things

Holy Father, my dear brothers,

The Church is as old as creation. In fact, in a certain sense, she is older than creation. "The world was created for the sake of the Church", say the Christians of the first centuries. The Church Fathers even speak of the preexistence of the Church. In the *Shepherd of Hermas*,[1] the Church appears as an old woman: "She existed before there was a world, and for her the world was created." "God created the world for the sake of communion with his divine life, a communion brought about by the 'convocation' of men in Christ, and this 'convocation' is the Church" (CCC 760). *Finis omnium Ecclesia*: the Church is the goal of all things. Some well-known words of Clement of Alexandria sum up this view: "Just as God's will is creation and is called 'the world,' so his intention is the salvation of men, and it is called 'the Church.' "[2]

[1] *Visio* 2, 4, 1.
[2] *Paedagogus* 1, 6, 27; CCC 760.

23

The Church is what God intended for creation, its real goal, which will only be reached when, as the Council, with the Church Fathers, says, "all the just from Adam onward, 'from Abel the just to the last of the elect', will be gathered together in the presence of the Father in the Church universal (*Ecclesia universalis*)" (LG 2). "In eternity God already saw 'the whole Christ' (*totus Christus*), the Church. In her he was well pleased. She is the masterpiece of his mercy. From the beginning of creation, God has been bringing all things to the fulfillment of his Christ."[3] If all things were "created for Christ" (cf. Col 1:16), then it is also true that all things were created for the Church, his Body (cf. Col 1:18).

This magnificent vision of the *universalis Ecclesia apud Patrem*, of the Church as the real goal of creation and of all that God does in creation, seems to contradict a much more modest view of the Church, which is also discernible in *Lumen Gentium*. Pope Pius XI had already said: "Men are not made for the Church but the Church for men."[4] Did the Second Vatican Council not use the image of a *serving Church*, which can radiate no other light than Christ's, a Church that, in a favorite image of the Church Fathers, is like the moon whose light derives totally from the sun: "Lumen gentium cum sit *Christus*".[5]

---

[3] Fr. Marie-Eugène de l'Enfant Jésus, *Je veux voir Jésus* (Venasque, 1988), 657.

[4] Allocution to the Lenten Preachers of Rome, February 28, 1927, cited in H. de Lubac, *The Splendor of the Church*, trans. Michael Mason (San Francisco: Ignatius Press, 1986), 65.

[5] Cf. Hugo Rahner, "Mysterium Lunae", in *Symbole der Kirche* (Salzburg: Muller, 1964).

The Church is *both* these things, *end* and *means*, the *final goal* of the plan of creation and at the same time "a kind of sacrament or *sign and instrument* of intimate union with God and of the unity of the whole human race" (LG 1). In the pilgrim Church the plan of creation already begins to become a reality; in the perfected Church it will have attained its goal. The perfected creation will be the perfected Church. Then will the true meaning of the Church be displayed: communion with God, communion among men in God. If we follow the Council and look at the Church from this perspective, then we can see that she is both the way and the destination. She is a sign but also what the sign signifies—or, as classical sacramental theology would say: the Church is *sacramentum* (sacred sign) and *res sacramenti* (sacred reality signified), yet in such a way that *everything* about her and in her that is sign is ordered, or should be ordered, to what is signified. In the meditations of this retreat we shall return again and again to this vital tension in the mystery of the Church: she is at once both way and destination, and she is both these things *in Christ*, whose Body and Bride she is, Christ who is himself "the Way, the Truth, and the Life".

Finis omnium Ecclesia. The Church is as wide as God's plan of creation. She is its "inner ground", as Karl Barth said in reference to the Covenant.[6] The first consequence of this is the fundamental importance of faith in creation for

---

[6] *Kirchliche Dogmatik* 3, 1, 41, 3.

the right understanding of the Church. Creation is the
first language God speaks. Without it the Word of God
remains a foreign tongue. That is why the *Catechism of
the Catholic Church* goes into detail about the importance
of catechesis on creation. In the years of radical change
after the Council, there was sometimes an alarming neglect of the doctrine of creation. Since then we can see
the beginnings of a new awareness of its importance. It
is becoming more and more clear that without the first
article of the Creed, belief "in the Creator of heaven and
earth", the other articles lack any foundation (CCC 199;
281).

The truth about creation and the Creator is the basis of
all the other truths of the faith. Without it, talk about the
Covenant, about the Torah, about the Incarnation of the
Son of God, about salvation and grace, about the Church
and her sacraments and the new creation, is truly "in-
credible". It must therefore be placed at the beginning of
evangelization, of the proclamation of the faith—if not in
chronological order, then in objective content. It was not
for nothing that the early Church began her baptismal catechesis with the reading of the account of creation. The
first step to conversion is faith in the one God, the Creator
of heaven and earth.

We have an illustration of this in a strange story in the
Acts of the Apostles. During their first missionary jour-
ney, Paul and Barnabas come to the town of Lystra in
Asia Minor. There Paul heals a man crippled from birth.
The spontaneous reaction of the people was to cry out:
"The gods have come down to us in the likeness of men!"
(Acts 14:11). They call Barnabas Zeus, and Paul, because

he was the chief speaker, they call Hermes. The priest
of Zeus brings oxen and garlands and, with a crowd of
people, wants to offer sacrifice. What in the Areopagus
Paul will call—half in rebuke, half in praise—the piety
of the Athenians (cf. Acts 17:22), he meets here, not in
academic disputation, but in the robust form of popular
pagan religiosity.

The two apostles tear their garments and implore the
crowd to desist from such blasphemous actions:

> Men, why are you doing this? We also are [only] men, of
> like nature with you, and bring you good news, that you
> should turn from these vain things to a living God who
> made the heaven and the earth and the sea and all that is
> in them. In past generations he allowed all the nations to
> walk in their own ways; yet he did not leave himself with-
> out witness, for he did good and gave you from heaven
> rains and fruitful seasons, satisfying your hearts with food
> and gladness (Acts 14:8–18).

A strange missionary sermon from the Apostle of Jesus
Christ! No word about Jesus! No word about his gospel.
It is the only missionary discourse in which Christ is not
mentioned. The reason for that, of course, is the state
of the people being addressed. Where there is a lack of
belief in the one true God, Christ cannot be preached,
and the Church cannot be "planted".

In this scene, in the situation it describes, we are dealing with questions that are supremely metaphysical and
utterly existential. We are dealing with the fundamental
question of the constitution of reality, of being, of the
orientation of our existence as determining everything in
our lives.

"We also are [only] men, of like nature with you." These words represent a tremendous process of change, a revolution in thought and behavior. "We are only men", not demi-gods, nor the products of chance, but *creatures*. Faith in creation introduces a radical dividing line, a *diastema*, as Gregory of Nyssa puts it: the dividing line between uncreated and created being, between God who alone truly *is*, eternally and perfectly, and creation, which does not have its being and existence from itself. This dividing line is of fundamental significance. We can scarcely overrate its importance.

"We also are [only] men, of like nature with you." This insight is at once religious, metaphysical, and ethical. It is not purely theoretical. According to Paul, it demands "conversion", a complete turnaround: "Turn to the living God", who created heaven and earth. The acknowledgment of God as Creator and the acceptance of one's own creatureliness cannot take place without a turning away from the false gods that are mere "nothings" and turning toward the "living God". Conversion means being painfully cut loose from passionate dependencies, from the fascination of the gods, and being set free for truth and right relationship with God and the world. But Paul also points to two unmistakable signs in human hearts that show that this turning around, this conversion, is not an arbitrary command but something that meets the deepest yearning in the heart of man: *gratitude and joy*.

Paul refers to the simple way God speaks to us in his creation: "He did not leave himself without witness." He gives rains and fruitful seasons. He does good "from

heaven". And he bears witness to himself by speaking to
man in his heart: he satisfies your hearts with food and
joy. All these things are not *proofs* for the world's created-
ness, for our being creatures. But they are *pointers*, which
address the mind as well as the heart. "He did good and
gave you from heaven rains and fruitful seasons." By the
words "from heaven", Paul is referring to the *gratuitous-
ness* of the simple gifts of creation, such as rain and fruitfulness. They are gifts of heaven, "from above". The pagan world knew this well enough; our world is in danger
of forgetting it and must learn it anew! Only if we learn
again simple gratitude to the Giver of all gifts will the
ground be prepared for a fruitful reception of the gifts of
grace.

Gratitude and *joy* go hand in hand. Peter speaks of the
"unutterable joy" (1 Pet 1:8) given to those who love
Christ. The "nursery school" of such joy is the joy, mentioned by Paul, in the hearts of those who gratefully accept God's gifts in creation. This joy, growing out of gratitude in the human heart, is God's most reliable ally in
his dealings with man. In this joy, Saint Ignatius Loyola
would discover a reliable indicator for the discernment of
God's will, and on this foundation he builds his *Spiritual
Exercises*.

Finis omnium Ecclesia. The Church is foreshadowed in creation. Creation, therefore, serves the Church, comes to
assist her on her way, attains in her its fulfillment. In the
twelfth chapter of the Apocalypse, we are told that the

earth comes to the aid of the Woman in the wilderness by swallowing the river that the Dragon spewed out on the Woman in the wilderness in order to destroy her (Rev 12:15–16)—an image to show that the whole of creation is at the service of the beloved Bride, the Woman, the Church.

This image also shows, of course, that creation's help is for an oppressed, persecuted, martyred Church. On the other hand, it also shows that only in the mystery of the Church does creation find the healing for which it impatiently longs: "We know that the whole creation has been groaning in travail together until now" (Rom 8:22). The Church is the object of all creation's yearning, "for the creation was subjected to futility, not of its own will but by the will of him who subjected it in hope; because the creation itself will be set free from its bondage to decay and obtain the glorious liberty of the children of God" (Rom 8:20–21).

In the Church's liturgy, in her sacraments, in prayer, in the sanctification of life, in active love for the poor—in all these ways the healed creation is already present. The relationship of creation and the Church can be understood only in the light of the Easter mystery, the mystery of the Fall, the Incarnation, and the Redemption. Augustine calls the Church the "*mundus reconciliatus*", the reconciled world. In the meditations that follow, we shall return constantly to this way of reconciliation, which is the way and the goal of the Church.

Let us conclude with some words from the Catechism: "The Church is the goal of all things, and God permitted such painful upheavals as the angels' fall and man's sin only as occasions and means for displaying all the power of his arm and the whole measure of the love he wanted to give the world."[7]

PRAISED BE JESUS CHRIST!

[7] CCC 760; cf. Fr. Marie-Eugène de l'Enfant Jésus, *Je veux voir Jésus* 657.

Second Meditation
Heaven and Earth

The Church "was already present in figure at the beginning of the world" (LG 2), that is, the *whole* of creation, "heaven and earth", is a prefiguring of the Church. A sense of creatureliness, of what it means to be a creature, is, therefore, a prerequisite for a sense of the Church. We need the language of creation in order to be able to name the Church and her mystery. But the opposite is also true: we can only understand the language of creation in the light of the Church.

The next three meditations will try, in the light of the revealed mystery of the Church, to look at the prefiguring of the Church in the order of creation.[1] The first meditation considers the relationship of heaven and earth as the archetype of the two dimensions of the Church, which is at once "the earthly Church and the Church endowed with heavenly gifts" (LG 8). Then follows a special meditation on the *Ecclesia de angelis*, the world of the angels as a prefiguring of the Church. The next meditation will be devoted to the "grammar" of the visible creation, whose language the Church speaks. The final meditation is devoted to Divine Providence, that is, to

---

[1] Cf., for what follows, my lectures at the 1993 Salzburg university conference, in P. Gordan, ed., *Lob der Erde* (Graz, Vienna, and Cologne, Verlag Styria, 1994), 31–62.

the way in which God brings his plan for creation to its goal.

There was a time when a good many theologians thought they had to explain carefully that "heaven and earth" were part of an outdated picture of the world, in which there were an "above" and a "below". Such naively rationalistic "demythologizing" forgets that, whatever the picture of the world may look like, for man there will always be an "above" and a "below": the sky above us and the earth on which we live. Whoever looks with longing into the sky, whoever raises his hands in prayer, bears witness to a primordial fact, expressed in myths and symbols yet rooted in the earthly life of man: the earth is not everything but stands in a polarity with heaven. "In the one cosmos", says Karl Barth, "there is an above and a below. They only reflect—though they always reflect —the true, strict, and proper above and below of Creator and creature, of God and man."[2] The polarity and interconnection of heaven and earth are a symbol, an analogy, for the relationship of Creator and creature, an analogy for the Church.

"In the beginning God created the heavens and the earth" (Gen 1:1). With these words, both heaven and earth are placed in the category of creatureliness: heaven is as much created as earth. God is "above heaven and earth" (Ps 148:13). Both are his own property (1 Chron 29:11). And yet heaven is a kind of "sacrament" of God's sublimity and proximity: "For as the heavens are high above the earth, so great is his steadfast love toward those who fear him" (Ps 103:11).

---

[2] *Dogmatik* 3/3 (1950), 490f.

Earth is dependent on heaven. Rain and dew are signs of our dependence on the "above", whence "every good endowment and every perfect gift" comes down (James 1:17). The forgetting or suppressing of this very real dependence of our earthly life on heaven above is related to the deeper, graver forgetting of the radical dependence of creatures on the God of heaven and earth. This forgetfulness even affects the image of the Church. Nowadays there is a widespread disregard of "the Church of heaven", against the clear teaching of *Lumen Gentium* (chap. 7).

In the church of Sant'Ignazio in Rome, Andrea Pozzo fashioned a most splendid representation of the interconnection of heaven and earth—in the ceiling of the nave, a grandiose perspective of Baroque architecture, which opens up on an infinite Heaven. St. Ignatius soars upward toward the Blessed Trinity. Other saints of the Society of Jesus follow him. Angels ascend and descend, forming a bond with the allegories of the four continents, which strive with all their might toward the fellowship of heaven.

Does earth rise up to heaven? Does heaven come down to earth? Both movements are there. But the "above" completely determines the "below". It is the goal of its yearning, the place to which it journeys. And from "above" comes help for the Church on earth, the light that brightens her face. The homeland of the Church is "above". It is there that "our commonwealth" (Phil 3:20) is to be found.

Anxiety threatens to make us forgetful of the heavenly homeland of the Church—anxiety lest we be accused of "pie in the sky when you die", "the opium of the people", a lack of commitment to *this world*, to the earth. But when heaven no longer opens up above to reveal the fellowship of the angels and saints, the pilgrim Church becomes dreary and desolate; in fact, she forgets that she *is a pilgrim*, that she has the joy of journeying through trials and tribulations to the heavenly homeland.

One dimension of the polarity of heaven and earth should be given special mention here: the interconnection of the visible and invisible creation. This is of extraordinary importance for the Church. She is inconceivable without those glorious creatures that we call *angels*. Pre-Christian Jewish exegesis already interpreted God's creation of heaven and earth to mean that he created the world of the "heavenly hosts", the myriad spiritual, supermundane beings who are in his service. Paul is in this tradition, but he opens it up to Christ: "In him all things were created, in heaven and on earth, visible and invisible, whether thrones or dominions or principalities or powers" (Col 1:16). The creatures in heaven are the angels. They are part and parcel of the world of the Bible.

The earth has grown poorer, and so have we, since the widespread loss among Christians of a sense of the reality of God's invisible creatures. We always sing the *Sanctus* in harmony with the praises of the angels: What does that mean for our understanding of the celebration of the Eucharist? In the *Confiteor*, at the beginning of Mass, we ask Blessed Mary Ever-Virgin and all the *angels* and saints, as well as our brothers and sisters, to pray for us to God the Father Almighty: What does that mean for our understanding of penitence? People who like to think of the angels as mere symbols of fulfilled human beings really ought to delete these texts from the liturgy and not re-place them. That would be an honest solution to their problems.

But the angels are returning, and unfortunately so are the demons, in all kinds of forms—in New Age and An-throposophy, in the chaos of today's comics and rock mu-sic. We can confront this proliferation only if we reflect in faith on the nature and activity of these angelic crea-tures. Romano Guardini got to the heart of the matter. In a sermon on the Feast of the Holy Guardian Angels, he said:

> There is much that might be said in reply to the ques-tion about the significance of the angels. Jesus said the most important thing in a most sacred context, namely, in the prayer he taught his own. In its third petition we are supposed to ask God for his will to be done on earth as it is in heaven. Now it is the angels who do his will in heaven. We are told that they "always behold the face of the Father who is in heaven" (Mt 18:10). With loving vision, they understand the decrees of God's Providence and accomplish his will in pure obedience, with a splendid vigor and precision.

God's will is done completely in one place in creation, even when it is not done on earth: in heaven, in the world of the angels, of whom the saints are the com-panions. This is the magnificence and splendor of these creatures that they have permanently and perfectly dedi-cated their whole being to the will of God, in an act of their freedom that penetrates and completely takes hold of them: *Thy will be done.* Heaven is where this happens, and where it happens on earth as it is in heaven, then heaven has already come on earth. And where it does *not* happen, where the freedom of God's purely spiritual creatures, a freedom that can take hold of itself and give itself in an undivided act of the will, rejects the will of God, there is hell, and where that happens on earth, then earth becomes hell.

The angels lead us into the pure, light-filled world of the will of God. That is why in a special way they surround Christ; indeed, they are *his* angels. Their "place", their "homeland", is the One who eternally receives himself from the Father and gives himself back to the Father, the One who lives completely in the will of the Father. It is no accident that the life of Jesus is surrounded so explicitly by angels, from the Incarnation all the way to the Ascension, indeed all the way to the Second Coming of the Son of Man "with his angels" (Mt 13:41).

Especially touching is the closeness of the angel at the time of the Agony in the Garden, our Lord's final surrender of himself to the Father's will, even unto death. In "The Dream of Gerontius", *John Henry Newman* contemplates the Angel of the Agony. What a mystery, that a creature be allowed to console and strengthen the Creator in the hour of his mortal anguish! What an analogy for our closeness, by prayer and service, to Christ, who, as *Pascal* said, is in agony till the end of the world!

The great Christian masters of the spiritual life point out the multiple analogies between the invisible and visible creation. Thus they see in the *angelikos bios* the model for the life of the monk, indeed the model of every form of spiritual life. The angels are totally dedicated to God in contemplative vision, but they are also totally available to be sent wherever God wills. In their whole being, they are "ministering spirits" (Heb 1:14). Therein lie their dignity and their sanctity. In this respect they are models of perfect creatureliness, the image of the mission of the Church.

Communion with the angels in prayer and love maintains our awareness that creation is not restricted to the earth. Without the knowledge our faith gives us of the angels, the invisible dimension of creation is in danger of fading from our minds, and with that will fade the complementarity of heaven and earth, of the spiritual and the bodily, of nature and grace, which embraces the whole scope of creation.

Living communion with the angels guards us against forgetting the invisible dimension of the Church. Loving and venerating the angels increases within us a sense of the reality and proximity of grace. As M. J. Scheeben said: "A high reverence for grace brings with it a great veneration of the holy angels. . . . The more we in our weakness fear the loss of grace, the more profoundly must we commend ourselves to their protection, their defense." And Saint Thomas Aquinas once said: "The angels cooperate in all our good works."[3] The communion, established in the act of creation, between invisible and visible creatures, between the angels and the material cosmos (a truth of which the Christian Middle Ages had a deeper knowledge than our current rationalism), but also between angels and men, is truly a *praefiguratio* of the Church as the goal of the Creator.

PRAISED BE JESUS CHRIST!

---

[3] *Summa theologiae* 1a 114, 3, ad 3 (abbreviated hereafter as STh; CCC 350.

Third Meditation
The Visible World

The Council says: "The faithful must recognize the innermost nature of the whole of creation, its value and its ordering to the praise of God" (LG 36,2). The recognition of the nature of created being is necessary if we are to have the right attitude toward human thought and activity.

The exegesis of the first two chapters of Genesis is traditionally the "place" for the Christian doctrine of being, the school of Christian thinking. Here certain fundamental philosophical, metaphysical principles become a concrete reality. These principles are the chief presuppositions of the Christian doctrine of salvation. To understand the world as creation implies a certain understanding of being, a "metaphysics of creation". The biblical "six days" of creation were seen by the Doctors of the Christian tradition as a concrete unfolding of this "metaphysics of creation". Augustine and Basil, Bonaventure and Thomas, have bequeathed us detailed commentaries on the *hexaemeron*. However, neoscholastic theology largely neglected this theological topic. In our own century Karl Barth and Romano Guardini attempted theological expositions of the "six days", but they were more or less the only ones to do so.

This neglect is particularly evident in the catechetics of recent years. Too often a worry about coming into conflict with the natural sciences has held sway. Anxiety about another "Galileo case", together with disassociation from "fundamentalism", have led to the situation in which the first chapter of Genesis is usually read as the expression of an outdated world view rather than as a "catechesis on creation".

In its own catechesis on creation, the Catechism examines the *hexaemeron* in order to find the truths about creation, about created being, that it contains. The following comments, which adhere closely to the text of the Catechism (CCC 337–49), may help to show that here we face truly fundamental questions:

[CCC 338] The first doctrine to be considered, the one that determines everything else, is creation *ex nihilo* (CCC 296–98). "Nothing exists that does not owe its existence to God the Creator." We really cannot grasp deeply and seriously enough how far-reaching are the "consequences of faith in creation" (to quote the title of a paper by Joseph Cardinal Ratzinger), intellectually and philosophically as well as existentially. Some words spoken by Christ to Saint Catherine of Siena provide the "keynote" of this reflection: "Do you know, daughter, who you are and who I am? If you know these two things, you have beatitude in your grasp. You are she who is not, and I am He Who Is." According to her biographer, Blessed Raymond of Capua, everything else our Lord taught Catherine was summed up in this one fundamental experience.[1]

Created being is not a necessary emanation from the

---

[1] Raymond of Capua, *The Life of Catherine of Siena*, trans., intro.,

Divine Being or a degenerate part of that Being, but something freely thought and willed by God's wisdom and love. It is, therefore, in a position to be a "Thou" in relation to the Creator: "Thou art—I am". Seven *unfoldings* of this fundamental truth now follow in the Catechism. Each of them sheds light on one of its aspects. Each could be the subject of a meditation in its own right.

1. [339] "Each creature possesses its own particular goodness and perfection." Creatures are not random ports-of-call in the voyage of evolution. As the Council says,[2] they have their own God-willed being, their own "stability, truth, and excellence", their own laws and order. The Catechism stresses the ethical implications of this truth: "Man must therefore respect the particular goodness of every creature, to avoid any disordered use of things which would be in contempt of the Creator and would bring disastrous consequences for human beings and their environment" (CCC 339).

2. [340] "God wills the *interdependence of creatures*. . . . The spectacle of their countless diversities and inequalities tells us that no creature is self-sufficient. Creatures exist only in dependence on each other, to complete each other, in the service of each other" (CCC 340).

---

and annotated by Conleth Kearns, O.P. (Wilmington, Del.: Glazier, 1980), 85f.

[2] Pastoral Constitution on the Church in the Modern World, *Gaudium et spes* (December 7, 1965), no. 36, 2 (abbreviated hereafter as GS).

This applies to human beings, too, who are equal in dignity but highly different in their gifts: "These differences belong to God's plan, who wills that each receive what he needs from others" (CCC 1937).

Creaturely variety is not an accident, as Gnosticism assumes, or a fall from the One, as Neoplatonism thinks, but willed by God, an expression in many forms of the plenitude of the divine essence. It is in the *communio* of the Church, the *one* Body of Christ in many members, that this variety of created and supernatural gifts is able fully to unfold.

3. [341] "*The beauty of the universe:* The order and harmony of the created world results from the diversity of beings and from the relationships which exist among them. . . . The beauty of creation reflects the infinite beauty of the Creator and ought to inspire the respect and submission of man's intellect and will" (CCC 341). What is worthy of admiration is not just the order of the cosmos but rather its *intelligibility*. Einstein is supposed to have said that what is so amazing is not that we understand things but that they are *understandable*. They come from the light of Divine Reason, not from an anonymous chaos, and so they, too, are "bright" and "luminous" for the light of our reason. That is why the Church will always be the great defender of human reason and its God-given powers. And the good use of reason will always be the natural ally of faith.

4. [342] There is an order of ranks, a "hierarchy", among creatures. This reality is the foundation in creation for

the hierarchical constitution of the Church. The order of creation teaches us that hierarchy and communion are not in contradiction. "God loves all his creatures and takes care of each one, even the sparrow" (CCC 342). Every creature is valuable; each has its own perfection; all have creatureliness in common. "Nevertheless, Jesus said: 'You are of more value than many sparrows' (Lk 12:7), or again: 'Of how much more value is a man than a sheep!' (Mt 12:12)" (CCC 342). There is also a "hierarchy" among creatures who are equal in nature: we are reminded of this by, for example, the Fourth Commandment and, more generally, by the "order of love", the *ordo caritatis* (CCC 2197).

Reflection on the *ordo caritatis* seems to me one of the priorities of Catholic social doctrine today. (The Catechism contains quite a few references to it; cf. CCC 1934–38.) What is involved here is the *concrete* affirmation of the order of creation.

5. [343] "*Man is the summit* of the Creator's work." If there is a hierarchy among creatures, the hierarchy must have a summit. "[T]he inspired account expresses [this] by clearly distinguishing the creation of man from that of the other creatures" (CCC 343). Such biblical, Christian "anthropocentrism" is massively criticized these days. Many people complain that it is precisely *this* image of man that is responsible for the ecological catastrophe. Creation's "summit" has become its greatest threat. Man is nature's dangerous troublemaker. It would be better for nature if man did not exist.

By contrast, *Gaudium et spes* says with great confidence: "Man is the only creature on earth . . . that God has willed for its own sake" (GS 24,3). This implies another statement: "There is almost unanimous agreement between believers and non-believers that everything on earth is ordered to man as its center and summit" (GS 12,1). Today this quasi unanimity is all but nonexistent. The problems are not new. Ridicule of the Christian view of man as "summit of creation" was well known in antiquity. There is a popular saying that man's arrogant assertion of his superiority to the animals is shameful. More troubling still is the question Pascal asks himself: What is man in the face of the limitless cosmos?

Modernity is marked by both attitudes: on the one hand, the limitless self-glorification of man; on the other hand, the radical reduction of man. In the cathedral on the Wawel in Krakow, the Renaissance Master of the Sigismund Chapel inscribed on the cupola, not the name of God, as was usual elsewhere, but his own. And he calls himself "*facto*"—creator! Man has become creator. At the end of this exaltation of man as creator of himself stands the "machine man" (*homme machine*), man reduced to mechanism, to mere product, to "human material". Robert Spaemann sums it up in a short phrase: Man becomes an anthropomorphism.

Common to both tendencies is the loss from view of the *creatureliness of man*. It becomes clearer and clearer that *everything*, including the basis of our view of man, depends on the *first article of the Creed*, on faith in the one God, the Father, the Creator, just as *all* authentic human conduct depends on obedience to the first of the Ten Commandments (CCC 199).

It is vital to arouse and to foster a sense, a feeling, for the creatureliness of man. In *Gaudium et spes* the Council has given us the Magna Charta of the Christian view of man, a vision of man that is at once sober and inspiring. "*Sobria ebrietate*", in the "sober drunkenness" of the Holy Spirit, we must proclaim this vision of man's grandeur and dignity, of the threats upon him and the vocation before him, but above all we must try to *live* the vision.

The heart of this anthropology is the doctrine that man is created "in the image of God" (GS 12,3). The unfolding of the Council's anthropology is one of the great tasks of today. The catecheses of the Holy Father have shown us how the great themes of *Gaudium et spes* should be taken up and developed: the unity of man in body and soul; the communion of persons; "male and female he created them"; reason, conscience, and freedom; the drama of sin; the enigma of death; above all the light of Christ, in whom alone the mystery of man truly becomes clear (GS 12–22). Without presumption and arrogance, with great gratitude, we can confess that here the Church bears a costly treasure "in earthen vessels", a treasure that she is called to open up and share with today's world.

There is much that ought to be said about this great vision of man. One point at least should be made. It appears constantly in the Catechism as one of its fundamental ideas: "Because of its common origin *the human race forms a unity*" (CCC 360; cf. 225, 404, 775, 831, 842). In his encyclical of October 20, 1939, Pope Pius XII based his unequivocal No to Nazi racism on this doctrine. *Lumen Gentium* presents the Church to us as a sacrament, that is to say, as a sign and instrument of the unity of the human race (cf. LG 1). In the following quotation from Pope Pius XII's encyclical it becomes clear that the Church was already prefigured in the origins of creation, from the very beginning of the human race:

> O wondrous vision, which makes us contemplate the human race in the unity of its origin in God . . . in the unity of its nature, composed equally in all men of a material body and a spiritual soul; in the unity of its immediate end and its mission in the world; in the unity of its dwelling, the earth, whose benefits all men, by right of nature, may use to sustain and develop life; in the unity of its supernatural end: God himself, to whom all ought to tend; in the unity of the means for attaining this end; . . . in the unity of the redemption wrought by Christ for all.[3]

" 'This law of human solidarity and charity,' without excluding the rich variety of persons, cultures, and peoples, assures us that all men are truly brethren" (CCC 361). The family of man is created and called to become the *familia Dei*, the family of God. The solidarity of a common origin is not limited to the community of the human family. It has an even more inclusive dimension, to which the Catechism's catechesis on the *hexaemeron* refers and with which we shall now conclude.

6. [344] The "work of the six days" also means that "there is a *solidarity among all creatures* arising from the

---

[3] Pius XII, encyclical *Summi pontificatus*, no. 3; CCC 360.

fact that all have the same Creator and are all ordered to his glory" (CCC 344). This all-embracing solidarity of creation prefigures the new creation that is already present in "seed and . . . beginning" (LG 5) in the Church. Many people today are trying to overcome modernity's Cartesian separation of the *res cogitans* from the *res extensae*, of the human mind from the world. The trouble is that they are doing this because they want man to be absorbed into the great totality of the cosmos. The Catechism shows the true Christian way of solidarity with creation in Saint Francis' "Canticle of the Sun": he praises God "in all [his] creatures", recognizes that he has a kinship with Brother Sun and Sister Moon, and with them serves God in creaturely devotion and "all humility" ("e ringraziate e serviteli cun grande umiltate", CCC 344).

7. [345] The whole of creation points beyond itself to its final destiny in the Church (cf. CCC 345). This is shown by the fact that the whole "work of the six days" is directed toward the Sabbath as its proper end: "On the seventh day God finished his work which he had done" (Gen 2:1). The Catechism draws three conclusions from this ordination of creation to the Sabbath:

a. Creation is waiting for its definitive Sabbath, its completion in the Kingdom of God. And yet God's work is already "complete". It has its foundation, its proper order and laws, which are signs of the faithfulness of God's covenant. "If I have not established my covenant with day and night and the ordinances of heaven and earth, then I will reject the descendants of Jacob and David my servant" (Jer 33:25–26). Not without reason do we pray:

"*Our help* is in the name of the Lord, who created heaven and earth." If God is as faithful to his covenant as he is to his creation, then our fidelity to his covenant means that we have an obligation to respect his creation and its ordinances (cf. CCC 346).

b. "Creation was fashioned with a view to the sabbath and therefore for the worship and adoration of God. Worship is inscribed in the order of creation. As the rule of Saint Benedict says, nothing should take precedence over 'the work of God,' that is, solemn worship" (CCC 347). Israel already knew that creation did not exist for itself. Its goal is the glorification of God, in which the happiness of man and all creation is to be found. "The world", the Catechism reminds us, quoting the First Vatican Council, "was made for the glory of God" (CCC 293), words that are then explained with the help of Saint Bonaventure: "not to increase his glory, but to show it forth and to communicate it" (ibid.).

c. The Sabbath also represents a *liberation*. After the six days of creation, God rested and "was refreshed" (Ex 31:17). That is why man, too, ought to rest from his work and let other people, especially the poor, be "refreshed" (Ex 23:12; cf. CCC 2172). The Sabbath is thus closely connected with *the* great liberation, the exodus from slavery in Egypt. And here, too, we find a *praefiguratio* of the Church: the Church will be the place of rest promised by the Lord, the realm of liberation from the yoke of slavery to sin.

Here we catch an echo of a theme that hitherto has been silent, a theme that henceforth will constantly keep us company: the question of evil and of deliverance from its power. Before we turn to this subject tomorrow, we shall conclude our meditation on creation with some words about the Providence of God.

PRAISED BE JESUS CHRIST!

Fourth Meditation
"God Carries Out His Plan: Divine Providence" (CCC 302)

In 1273, one year before his death, Saint Thomas Aquinas preached some sermons in Naples, in the local dialect, on the Apostles' Creed (*Collationes in symbolum apostolorum*). His sermon on the first article of the Creed begins with these words:

> The first of all the articles of faith is that the faithful must believe in one God. . . . It will be well to consider what is meant by this word "God", for it signifies the governor and provider of all things. To believe there is a God is to believe in One whose government and providence extend to all things, whereas one who believes that all things happen by chance does not believe there is a God.[1]

Believing in God is inseparable from believing in his Providence. Believing in God the Creator is possible only if he is believed in also as "governor and provider" of his creation. Now ruling and guiding means: leading something to its goal. God leads creation to its goal, to its fulfillment: to the Kingdom of God, to the "Church universal in the presence of the Father (*universalis Ecclesia apud*

---

[1] St. Thomas Aquinas, *The Three Greatest Prayers: Commentaries on the Lord's Prayer, the Hail Mary, and the Apostles' Creed* (Manchester, N.H.: Sophia Institute Press, 1990), 8.

Patrem)" (LG 2), the perfect communion of the just with the triune God. "We call *'divine providence'* the dispositions by which God guides his creation toward this perfection" (CCC 302). "By his providence", says the First Vatican Council, "God protects and governs all things which he has made" (CCC 302).

Apart from the resurrection of the body, there is no doctrine of the faith more intensely discussed in the theology and preaching of the early Church than the theme of *Divine Providence.* Pagan antiquity knew at best of a universal Divine Providence. The idea that the deity should trouble itself with individuals and concrete things was alien to the mind of ancient man. Belief in fate, an inescapable fate encompassing both gods and men, weighed down upon all. The unanimous testimony of Scripture has a very different message: "[T]he solicitude of divine providence is *concrete* and *immediate*; God cares for all, from the least things to the great events of the world and its history" (CCC 303).

Saint Thomas sums it up clearly and unequivocally: "Just as nothing can exist that is not created by God, so nothing can exist that is not subject to his government."[2] This is without doubt the decisive test for faith in creation: the assumption that creation as a whole and in each of its parts, immediately and at all times, is in the hands of God: "Our God is in the heavens; he does whatever he pleases" (Ps 115:3).

Faith in the absolute sovereignty of God is boundlessly consoling. It fills the hearts of *all* the saints. The Cate-

---

[2] STh 1a 103, 5.

chism presents us with two testimonies, from the two *women* Doctors of the Church (the only ones so far).[3] The first is some words of Saint Catherine of Siena: "*Everything* comes from love, all is ordained for the salvation of man, God does nothing without this goal in mind" (CCC 313). The other is the famous "bookmark" of Saint Teresa of Avila:

> Let nothing trouble you / Let nothing frighten you
> Everything passes / God never changes
> Patience / Obtains all
> Whoever has God / Wants for nothing
> God alone is enough (CCC 227).

We do not know what God is, but we do know that he is. We do not know *how* God's Providence does its work, but we do know *that* he brings everything to its final goal. We do not know the ways of God's Providence in advance, but we do believe that none of our ways lies outside of his Providence. In 1955 Pope Pius XII said this to an audience of historians: "The Catholic Church knows that all the events of history take place according to the will or permission of Divine Providence and that in history God fulfills his purposes."

In what follows, we shall consider this wonderful and essential truth about God's sovereign Providence in three aspects, each of which is a *praefiguratio* of the Church:

a. God's primary causality—the secondary causality of creatures;

---

[3] They have since been joined by St. Thérèse of Lisieux, whom Pope John Paul II declared a Doctor of the Church on October 19, 1997.

b. Providence and prayer;

c. Providence and suffering.

a. God is at work in all things—His creatures are at work in their own right

Saint Thérèse of Lisieux, whom Pope Pius XI called "the greatest saint of the modern age", and who may be declared a Doctor of the Church (twenty-five episcopal conferences have already petitioned it from the Holy Father),[4] once said: "God needs no one . . . to do good on earth."[5] But she also said: "Almighty God loves to show His power by making use of nothing."[6] She said: "Jesus needs no one to do His work."[7] But she also said: "He uses the weakest instruments to work wonders."[8]

God works in a sovereign way. With him nothing is impossible (cf. Lk 1:37; Mt 19:26). But can the creature do anything? Or is God the sole universal cause, the only truly efficient cause? This question touches upon the deepest level of the dignity of the creature, especially of the dignity of man, but at the same time it touches upon the very foundations of the Church and her activity.

The answer of Saint Thomas is of enormous importance: God grants his creatures not only to *exist* but also to *act*, each in its own way. It is precisely here that we see the incomparable majesty of the creative activity of God:

[4] See previous footnote.
[5] *Autobiographical Writings*, Manuscript C, 3v.
[6] *Lettres*, no. 220 (February 24, 1897).
[7] Ibid., no. 221 (March 19, 1897).
[8] Ibid., no. 201 (November 1, 1896).

he gives every creature its own being and sustains it, as the special being it is, in what it is and in what it becomes. "God grants His creatures not only their existence, but also the dignity of acting on their own, of being causes and principles for each other, and thus of cooperating in the accomplishment of his plan" (CCC 306).

We can see this especially in human freedom, that wonder of divine creation. Paul says: "Work out your own salvation with fear and trembling; *for* God is at work in you, both to will and to work for his good pleasure" (Phil 2:12–13). What a paradox, that *we* should work, because *God* is at work within us! At the level of pure reason, this interconnection of divine and human freedom is impenetrable. And yet there are some ways toward understanding it.

We find *one* of these in a surprising place in the Catechism: in the third part, in the chapter on human society, where we read:

> God has not willed to reserve to himself all exercise of power. He entrusts to every creature the functions it is capable of performing, according to the capacities of its own nature. This mode of governance ought to be followed in social life. The way God acts in governing the world, which bears witness to such great regard for human freedom, should inspire the wisdom of those who govern human communities. They should behave as ministers of divine providence (CCC 1884).

Christian social doctrine sets its standards by the "conduct" of God, whose Providence operates precisely by willing and effecting the proper operations of his creatures. The *principle of subsidiarity* is *one* concrete application of the way Divine Providence does its work. Respect for freedom is another. *Here*, in this vision of human freedom as willed and sustained by God, we find the roots of *Christian humanism*. Saint Thomas provides its classical and clearest expression: "The greater the perfection communicated by the governor to the governed, the better the government." Thomas gives the following explanation. The best kind of teacher is one who not only teaches his pupils but makes them teachers of others.[9] In other words, God's creative activity and Providence are at their most perfect when they produce creatures as much like the Creator as possible. We are back to the doctrine of the image of God.

We can say this, then: It is God's joy when his creatures display their own activity. God's Providence shows its perfection when it produces "provident beings". The Creator shines brightest in the *creative creature*. The Creator is not magnified when his creatures are belittled. Against such a false "exaltation" of God, Thomas says: "To detract from the perfection of creatures is to detract from the perfection of the power of God. . . . To deny things their proper activity is to disparage the goodness of God."[10]

Conversely, anyone who feels joy at the works of God's creatures, at their perfection, gives praise to the Creator and his Providence. Simple delight in a good meal, admiration for the work of a master craftsman, being deeply sat-

[9] Cf. STh 1a 103, 6.
[10] *Summa contra Gentiles* 3, 69.

isfied at success in one's work, being moved by some self-forgetful gesture of kindness: in all these things, whether or not it is recognized, shines out the splendor of the Creator in the works of his creatures. The man who knows the joy of this experience knows what I am talking about. The taste of such joy is unmistakable. Of this joy the Church is *mater et magistra.* Her life depends upon a full affirmation of creatureliness, and she is not ashamed of the sensible delight of her faith in the Creator. One of the great dangers in our time is the deadened sensitivity that is no longer capable of this simple joy.

Believing in the Creator also means believing in the great things he expects of his creatures. It seems to me that the deepest crisis in the Church today is that we no longer dare to believe in what God can do for the good with those who love him (cf. Rom 8:28). The spiritual masters traditionally call this torpor of mind and heart *acedia*, spiritual inertia, that "stagnation of the soul" (as Evagrius calls it) that paints the world and one's own life a dreary gray and robs everything of its taste and sparkle. The chief reason why there is so much gloom around in the Church today is that we do not respond generously to the bold challenges of God and fail to let ourselves be used, with all we are and all we have, as his coworkers (cf. 1 Cor 3:9). The creature can never know a greater self-fulfillment than letting himself be totally used by God.

b. Providence and prayer

God not only entrusts us with freedom and our own works but also expects of us greater things than we can do by ourselves. He asks us to cooperate in *his* works, far beyond what we ourselves can do. Again let us turn to Saint Thérèse, who expresses this truth in an incomparably clear way:

> It was one day when I was thinking of what I could do to save souls, a word of the gospel gave me a real light. In days gone by, Jesus said to His disciples when showing them the fields of ripe corn: "Lift up your eyes and see how the fields are already white enough to be harvested" (Jn 4:35), and a little later: "In truth, the harvest is abundant but the number of laborers is small, ask then the master of the harvest to send laborers" (Mt 9:37–38). What a mystery! . . . Is not Jesus all-powerful? Are not creatures His who made them? Why, then, does Jesus say: "Ask the Lord of the harvest that he send some workers?" Why? . . . Ah! it is because Jesus has so incomprehensible a love for us that He wills that we have a share with Him in the salvation of souls. He wills to do nothing without us. The Creator of the universe awaits the prayer of a poor little soul to save other souls redeemed like it at the price of all His Blood.[11]

By our actions, by the good works we perform, we can cooperate with God's Providence. By our prayer we can work with God so that he does something greater than we could ever attain. "He wills to do *nothing without us*." *Through us* and *with us*, he wants to do great things. In his *Pensées*, *Blaise Pascal* says: "Why did God institute prayer? To give his creatures the dignity of causality."

---

[11] St. Thérèse of Lisieux, *Lettres*, no. 135 (August 15, 1892); *General Correspondence*, vol. 2, 1890–1897, trans. by John Clarke, O.C.D. (Washington, D.C.: Institute of Carmelite Studies, 1988), 753.

Saint Thomas explains this in his long *quaestio* on prayer. There are things we can do because it is in our power to do them. There are other things that, though not in our power to do, can still be done by us when we ask that they be done by someone who can do them. *Petitionary prayer*, therefore, is, for Thomas, the primary form of prayer. It shows that we are *in need*, that we depend upon God. It is also the recognition that God really can *achieve* what we can only *request*. That is why petitionary prayer always has an element of adoration, of praise and thanksgiving to God.

Once more let us bring in Saint Thérèse. I am thinking of her prayers for the man she called "my first child" —Pranzini, the triple murderer. She implored God for the grace of his conversion. In fact, she was *certain* of it because of her *total confidence* in the "infinite mercy of Jesus". Pranzini went to the guillotine without any sign of repentance. Then suddenly he seized the crucifix and kissed the wounds of Jesus three times. Strengthened by this *sign* for which she had prayed, Thérèse was powerfully moved by the desire to "save souls".[12] Thus the Little Flower's prayer becomes a cooperation with God's saving plan. It is more than her own doing. God wants us to cooperate with him. "The Creator of the universe awaits the prayer of a poor little soul to save other souls."

c. Providence and suffering

I shall never forget something that took place during the Extraordinary Synod of Bishops in 1985 (when an appeal

---

[12] *Autobiographical Writings*, Manuscript A, 45v–46v.

was made to the Holy Father for the Catechism). On November 28, the venerable Cardinal Tomašek made a speech. He concluded with these words:

> *Dobbiamo lavorare per il Regno di Dio, il che è molto; pregare per il Regno, il che vale di più; dobbiamo soffrire con Cristo Crocifisso per il Regno di Dio, il che è tutto.* [We must work for the Kingdom of God—that is a great thing. We must pray for the Kingdom—that is more important still. We must suffer for the Kingdom with the Crucified Christ —that is everything.]

When he had finished, everyone spontaneously rose to their feet and applauded this confessor of the faith.

Working, praying, suffering—in that order! Here we meet the mystery of suffering, the mystery of the Cross. Why is this the "be all and end all" of cooperation with God's Kingdom, in the realization of God's plans? What is the role played in this plan by moral and physical evil, by suffering? How did suffering get into God's good creation? Why did God allow it? And why does the way to the Church, as the destination of the ways of God, lead us through the Cross? This question will constantly come up in our meditations during the next few days. Let us conclude this first day, dedicated to God's plan of creation as a *praefiguratio* of the Church, with these words of Jean Cardinal Daniélou:

> God created us only so that we could share in His joy. If it were not true that God created us so that we could share eternally in His life, existence would have absolutely no meaning; the world would be absurd. It is only in faith in the intentions of God's love that the world finds its

meaning. The world has no other justification than its having been destined in Christ for divine beatitude. This is the response to all those who would object that "a good God would not have been able to create a world so full of misery and suffering." St. Paul responds that it is through this that God seeks to build—and will irrevocably and ultimately succeed in building—the city of God in which His children will be bathed in the light of the Trinity.[13]

PRAISED BE JESUS CHRIST!

[13] Jean Daniélou, *Prayer: The Mission of the Church*, trans. David Louis Schindler, Jr. (Grand Rapids, Mich.: W. B. Eerdmans, 1996), 87.

THE CHURCH—PREPARED FOR IN THE OLD COVENANT

First Meditation
Whence Comes Evil?

Without the drama of sin we cannot understand the meaning of the Church. Only against the background of the rupture through sin of man's original communion with God and with his fellowman can we see why God's plan to give his creatures a share in his life takes the concrete form of election and therefore selection.

As Cardinal Daniélou says:

> God's plan has crossed through the drama of evil and sin. And if evil and sin are able to hinder this plan, they will nevertheless fail to foil it. God, who introduced the first man and the first woman into Paradise—that is, into His beatitude—pursues His goal through the drama of sin by introducing the Sacrifice of His Son. The mystery of creation becomes the mystery of redemption because of this conflict between love's intentions and the resistance of evil.[1]

---

[1] Jean Daniélou, *Prayer: The Mission of the Church*, trans. David Louis Schindler, Jr. (Grand Rapids, Mich.: W. B. Eerdmans, 1996), 87.

The "preparation" for the Church began at the moment when man by his sin lost friendship with God. "The gathering together of the Church is, as it were, God's reaction to the chaos provoked by sin" (CCC 761). The different ways God has gathered mankind together are the theme of this second day of our retreat. First, we shall consider the drama of the sin of Adam, then the promises and paths of the *protoevangelium*, the covenant with Noah, and finally the history of God's love in the Old Covenant, a covenant he has never revoked.

We shall look, not just at the past, but also at the Church's *permanent* dimensions. After all, it is one and the same Church that was foreshadowed in creation, prepared for in the Old Covenant, and instituted in the fullness of time. All the "strata" of the Church's constitution remain present throughout her history, just as in the life of an individual the order of creation, the time of preparation, and the time of maturity have a permanent and simultaneous existence. In today's meditations we are, so to speak, in the *Advent of the Church*. May these meditations reawaken within us a *longing* for the Redeemer and also a feeling for the signs of his advent in our time, in the life of men and of nations.

The mystery of original sin (peccatum originale). "Unde malum?" asked Augustine in his *Confessions*.[2] Whence comes evil? To this primordial question of mankind no

[2] *Confessiones* 7, 7, 11.

human seeking and researching can find a complete answer. The "mystery of iniquity" (cf. 2 Th 2:7) is only illuminated by the "mystery of faith" (cf. 1 Tim 3:16). "We must therefore approach the question of the origin of evil by fixing the eyes of our faith on him who alone is its conqueror" (CCC 385).

The reality of original sin is not accessible to historical research or philosophical analysis. It is a revealed truth, which as such eludes investigation, even though it sheds light on many human experiences and helps us to understand them better. The true proportions, the full dimensions, of original sin can only be measured by the yardstick of Christ. "We must know Christ as the source of grace in order to know Adam as the source of sin. The Spirit-Paraclete, sent by the risen Christ, came to 'convict the world concerning sin' (Jn 16:8), by revealing him who is its Redeemer" (CCC 388). The realization that there is salvation only in the name of Jesus, and that he is the Savior of all men, makes us aware of the full consequences of original sin, "that all need salvation, and that salvation is offered to all through Christ" (CCC 389). The Catechism insists: "The Church, which has the mind of Christ (cf. 1 Cor 2:16), knows very well that we cannot tamper with the revelation of original sin without undermining the mystery of Christ" (CCC 389).

We are dealing here with a crucial point for our faith and life, with the certainty that the act of obedience of the *One* Man affects all men without exception, every man who has ever lived, who is alive, or who will live —indeed, the certainty that all men are contained and included *in the One* Man.

How can the action of *one* man have *such* consequences for *all* men? Here we reach the very foundations of the Christian doctrine of redemption. If Christ's death and Resurrection are to be more than just an example for us, if they are *the* divine act of atonement, embracing all times and ages, then this one act must reach out to *all* men. How else could we pray: "We adore thee, O Christ, and we bless thee, because by *thy* Holy Cross thou hast redeemed the *whole* world"? Or how could we say the words of Eucharistic Prayer III: "Lord, may this sacrifice, which has made our peace with you, advance the peace and salvation of *all the world*"? We are talking here about the universality of Christ, about his uniqueness as the one Mediator.

Human solidarity is insufficient as an explanation of how Jesus can achieve salvation for all men. It is because God established him as *Head* of mankind, because all things were created "through him and for him", because "He is before all things, and in him all things hold together" (Col 1:16–17), that all mankind is contained and included in the act of his obedience "unto death, even death on a cross" (Phil 2:8). Thus God is able to fulfill the plan of his good pleasure "to sum up all things under Christ as Head" (Eph 1:10)—through the Church, which is his Body.

Now is it simply a theological deduction to assume that, in similar fashion, the act of disobedience of *one* man can have disastrous consequences for *all* men? Is it *fundamentalism* to accept the idea of a *real* deed on the part of our first parents? It would be fundamentalism to take the symbolic language of the Bible literally. But it is something entirely different to accept the validity and truth of the Bible's unanimous conviction of faith that the human race forms *one* family, with the same nature and a common origin (cf. Gen 3:20; 5:1–2; 1 Chron 1:1; Wis 10:1; Job 15:7; Sir 49:17; Malachi 2:15; Tob 8:6; Acts 17:26). This presupposition is a *prerequisite* for the doctrine of original sin as well as for the certainty of the equal dignity of *all* men.

However, to understand original sin, we need another fundamental biblical concept: the idea that in our first parents, Adam and Eve, the whole human race is "as one body of one man".[3] The vocation of Adam and Eve is not just an individual one; it contains and includes *all* their successors as the members of *one* body. The fate of all mankind hinged on the "testing of their freedom" (cf. CCC 396) by the divine commandment. That is why their personal sin affected the whole of mankind contained in their loins. That is why all men come into this world as "exsules filii Hevae", poor banished children of Eve (*Salve Regina*). What our first parents lost, all their children lack, and that lack we call "original sin".

The *analogy of faith* can help us understand the consequences for *all* men of the vocation of *one* man. The Annunciation to Mary was the unique moment when God placed the whole weight of human history in the hands of *one* person. Saint Bernard of Clairvaux has given us a magnificent meditation on this moment in one of his sermons on the text "Missus est angelus Gabriel".[4] Breathless with suspense and full of hope, the whole of creation

---

[3] St. Thomas Aquinas, *De Malo* 4, 1; CCC 404.
[4] St. Bernard of Clairvaux, *Homilia super missus est*, 4, 8.

fixes its eyes on Mary and begs her to give that word of consent on which the fate of all men depends. Saint Thomas Aquinas adds this comment: "Through the angel's annunciation the consent of the Virgin Mary was expected in the name of all human nature."[5] The *realism* of this moment is probably the most striking analogy of faith for understanding the vocation of our first parents. The destiny of the whole human family hinges, in a historically concrete way, on Mary.

Here we touch upon an axiom of the works of God, an axiom of radical importance for the Church: God works through *individual*, particular human beings, in order to reach out to *all*. The destiny of mankind is never just the blind game of anonymous forces. Precisely because creation itself is a heritage destined for man, a call addressed by the Creator to the freedom of his creatures, the destiny of creation depends decisively on the free *Yes* of creatures. The doctrine of original sin (together with the doctrine of Redemption) confirms that history is always the history of a freedom that either makes a gift of itself or refuses to make a gift of itself. The doctrine of original sin is the guaranteed protection of the Christian *doctrine of freedom*.

The acceptance of the primordial sin of our first parents as a real, free action presupposes their actual existence. The existence of Adam and Eve is inaccessible to the historian. Archaeology or paleontology will never discover them. The original splendor of their human life in friend-

---

[5] STh 3a 30, 1; CCC 511.

ship with God is no longer accessible to our eyes darkened and bedimmed by original sin.

The saints give us a sense of what this original glory was like, even though we know of no human being who does not bear the disfiguring scars of sin. Mary is the only exception. "Tota pulchra es, Maria" (All fair art thou, O Mary), sings the liturgy (I can't help thinking of the incomparably lovely motets of Bruckner!). Here lies one of the meanings of the dogma of the *Immaculata*: in Mary we see, gazing across countless generations, the face of woman as God created her: Eve, the Mother of all the living. Is this not one of the reasons for the irresistible attraction that Mary has exerted everywhere throughout the earth?

The dogma of original sin is of inestimable importance for the whole structure of the faith. It would be valuable to show this in detail, in the different areas of the doctrine of the faith. One could show its importance for the doctrine of man, along the lines of Pascal's famous assertion: "Nothing gives us a rougher shock than this doctrine, and yet without this most incomprehensible of mysteries we are incomprehensible to ourselves. . . . The incomprehensibility of man without this mystery is greater than the incomprehensibility of this mystery to man."[6] It would be good to unfold the vast implications of the doctrine of original sin for the Church's social doctrine, as *Centesimus annus* points out: "The social order will be all the

---

[6] *Pensées*, no. 434.

firmer for taking this fact into account."[7] The ideologies, with their promises of an earthly paradise, have brought nothing but misery, as this "century of the wolves" has proved.[8]

There is *one* aspect of original sin that I should like to address in some detail, and that is the inner connection between the *dogma of original sin* and our *understanding of the Church*. I owe this insight to Robert Spaemann:

> The concept of the "People of God", which has been given so much attention since the Second Vatican Council, seems to me to be indirectly helpful for a new understanding of original sin. We have grown more aware that we exist in a solidarity and community of mutual help, that no one owes salvation to himself.

We *all* owe salvation to the sacrifice of Christ. We all need salvation, because we are all embroiled in guilt. Now this collective embroilment in guilt must not be misunderstood:

> [It does not mean] that mankind is a kind of solidarity and community of guilt. No, it means the exact opposite: because of the sin committed at the beginning of human history, mankind has *ceased to be a community of solidarity*. "Once you were no people", says Saint Peter (1 Pet 2:10), and Isaiah, whom Peter is quoting, adds: "All we like sheep have gone astray" (Is 53:6).
>
> Original sin is not a positive quality inherited by each man from his forefathers, but rather the lack of a qual-

---

[7] John Paul II, encyclical *Centesimus annus* (May 1, 1991), no. 25.

[8] *Jahrhundert der Wölfe* (The century of the wolves) is the title of the German translation of the memoirs of Nadezhda Mandelshtam, published in English as *Hope against Hope* (New York: Atheneum, 1970).

ity that he should have inherited. This missing quality is membership in a community of salvation. Mankind is no longer such a community of salvation. Birth into humanity is not birth into a community of salvation, into the People of God. In the case of a quality appropriate to the individual, one can reasonably ask why it is not given to one man just because another man lacks it. But the quality of membership in the People of God, a People that transmits salvation, cannot be passed on when this People does not even exist. One can interpret original sin, therefore, as the initial state of not belonging to the People of God. Membership in the new People of God does not happen through birth into the relationships of natural life but through faith and sacrament. Potentially, the new People of God is identical with the whole of mankind, but actually, it is the exact opposite—it is extracted out of mankind. That is why the Apostle Peter begins his preaching with the cry, "Save yourselves from this crooked generation!" (Acts 2:40).[9]

This helpful interpretation of original sin corresponds exactly with the core idea of the Council's teaching on the People of God, which begins with these words: "At all times and in every race, anyone who fears God and does what is right has been acceptable to him. He has, however, willed to make men holy and save them, not as individuals without any bond or link between them, but rather to make *them into a people* who might acknowledge him and serve him in holiness" (LG 9).

[9] In Christoph Schönborn, Albert Görres and Robert Spaemann, *Zur kirchlichen Erbsündenlehre* (Einsiedeln-Freiburg: Johannes, 1991), 63–64.

We shall look at the various stages of this "making into a people", of this formation of the *familia Dei*, in the meditations that follow.

PRAISED BE JESUS CHRIST!

Second Meditation
The "Protoevangelium"

Holy Father, my dear brothers,

O holy Father, we praise thee, for thou art great, and all
thy works thou hast done in wisdom and charity. Man
hast thou made in thine image, and to him hast thou entrusted the care of the whole world, so that, serving thee
the Creator alone, he might have dominion over all creatures. And when he disobeyed thee and lost thy friendship, thou didst not abandon him to the power of death,
for in thy mercy thou didst help all men to seek thee and
to find thee.[1]

Our situation has two aspects: we have fallen under
"the power of death", yet God remains true to *himself*
and to *us*. Our situation is *pitiful*, yet God's *pity* finds
ways and means to help us to seek him and find him.
The three "stages" of this seeking and finding are to be
the themes of today's meditations: the *protoevangelium*, the
covenant with Noah, and the election of Israel. For the

---

[1] Eucharistic Prayer IV. [This is my own translation from the Latin
of the *Missale romanum*. I have not given the authorized ICEL version of the prayer, because it fails to translate the word *misericorditer*
("mercifully"). The official German text uses the phrase *voll Erbarmen*,
"full of pity". Cardinal Schönborn takes up and develops this theme
—TRANS.]

Christian, these are not merely past events, the prehistory of the Church, but realities that are permanently valid, even though they find their fulfillment in the Church of the New Covenant, a fulfillment that did not lie within their own powers. These meditations are particularly important because the Church herself is still *in statu viae*, on pilgrimage to her final goal, and she marches on in the midst of a world that is often far from being a *mundus reconciliatus*, far from finding its home in the *familia Dei*.

To a rationalistic, scientific mind, the story of the Fall and its consequences (Gen 3) may seem like just a mythical tale, a "primitive world view". And yet the longer we meditate on these words and reflect on human existence, the more frighteningly and shatteringly clear it becomes that "divine revelation is uncannily correct . . . even when it appears stupid to all the sciences".[2]

We shall address three undoubtedly dominant aspects of human life: the world of work according to God's judgment of the man; the world of the relationship of the sexes according to God's judgment of the woman; the situation of struggle between good and evil according to God's judgment of the serpent. In all three areas, we find a deep disturbance of human relationships but also a promise, a "First Gospel". As Christians, but especially as pastors, we are asked to look at events—history, the present, the situation of man—*in the light of revelation*, which, as Romano Guardini says, is "the only knowing subject".[3] Only a sober contemplation of what is told us

[2] Romano Guardini, *Der Anfang aller Dinge*, 2d ed. (Wurzburg: Im Werkbund-Verlag, 1965), 90.

[3] Ibid., 17.

in Genesis 3 about the fallen state of man enables us to see why *the Cross* was and is necessary, why the world and every man need redemption, but also it makes us realize that the mystery of grace is at work in the history of fallen mankind from the very beginning.

1. "Because you . . . have eaten of the tree of which I commanded you, 'You shall not eat of it,' cursed is the ground because of you; in toil you shall eat of it all the days of your life; thorns and thistles it shall bring forth to you; . . . till you return to the ground, for out of it you were taken; you are dust, and to dust you shall return" (Gen 3:17–19).

How different this sounds from all the optimism of progress! Backbreaking toil is man's lot, and the fruit of his toil is meager—"thorns and thistles". And at the end comes death. . . . Is this pessimism? Or is it, at the end of *this* century, a kind of liberation from all ideological delusions about progress?

The loss of friendship with God brings with it the loss of intimacy with the "earth", with the world. The earth becomes a stranger to man, even his enemy. Man carries his inner disharmony into the world, forces his sick and rebellious will upon nature, and so becomes the destroyer of the earth, which he was supposed to "till and keep" (Gen 2:15). At the same time, man becomes the ruled rather than the ruler: nature, over which he is meant to have dominion, takes revenge and becomes a threat to man. Man will always "get the worst of it", and at the end, remorselessly, comes death.

What about culture? Are things any better there? In

the short time of man's recorded history, has he not made some tremendous achievements? Do we not rightly praise his achievements in science, in art, in the whole culture of the last two to three millennia? And yet . . . Here too, when we look at things soberly, without the ideology of progress, the "thorns and thistles" are horrendous. How much misery lies behind all these cultural achievements? No work of man is free of shadows. Who can measure the misery of the slaves who built the pyramids? Think of the countless dead of the Gulag Archipelago, sacrificed for the "Construction of Socialism". And even in times of peace, for how many people is their daily work really the "fulfillment of their human existence", the unfolding of their personalities? Daily life is full of thorns. The struggle to keep a job is tough. The loss of a job is bitter and hard to bear.

Are not the greatest works of culture shot through with toil, pain, and guilt? Is there not frailty amidst all their grandeur? However glorious Saint Peter's basilica may be, the wounds of the Reformation, the divisions in faith, went deeply into this work and disturb our pleasure in its magnificence. So many projects are left incomplete, unfinished. So much failure lingers alongside the successes and achievements. So much effort lies forgotten in the unread books in our libraries. So much effort is spent without thanks in the countless labors of unnoticed blue-collar workers, white-collar workers, mothers.

And yet in man's obligation to work there lies a blessing from God, a *protoevangelium*, which remains valid for all times. When he was in Nazareth, Pope Paul VI spoke of the "severe and redeeming law of human work" (CCC

533). "Despite all this toil, in a sense precisely because of this toil, work is a blessing for man. . . . Work is a blessing for man, for his very existence as man, because it is through work that, in a certain way, he becomes 'more of a man'."[4] Diligence and industriousness can, therefore, be virtues, helping man toward the good.

Work brings people together, unites them in common undertakings, and so builds up community. Of course, the doctrine of original sin also reminds us that this building up of community is not a nicely continuous progress. Each generation, each individual has to bend anew to the yoke of work and struggle hard against lethargy and distaste. There will never be a "heaven on earth" in which this struggle with oneself, this cross of effort and toil, will be overcome. Work is not, of course, a meaningless torment of Sisyphus. "It can also be redemptive. By enduring the hardship of work in union with Jesus, the carpenter of Nazareth and the one crucified on Calvary, man collaborates in a certain fashion with the Son of God in his redemptive work" (CCC 2427).

2. When he passes judgment on the woman, God says: "I will greatly multiply your pain in childbearing; in pain you shall bring forth children, yet your desire shall be for your husband, and he shall rule over you" (Gen 3:16).

The disturbance caused by original sin to the relationships of man and woman is even deeper than its effects on labor and the works of man. *Here* more than anywhere else is the doctrine of original sin necessary for us to de-

---

[4] Pope John Paul II, encyclical *Laborem exercens* (September 14, 1981), nos. 9, 3.

termine the true origin of the disturbance of human life. Physiology and psychology, sociology and history, have sharpened our perception of the many causes of trouble in the relationship of the sexes. But its roots lie deeper. In the final analysis, the "battle of the sexes" originates in the continuing trauma of the first sin.

The first act of infidelity toward God has permanent effects on the relations of man and woman. The few lines in Genesis are of inexhaustible depth and living truth. The first sin does not lead to the solidarity of sinners among themselves. Infidelity toward God leads to man and woman's *betrayal of each other*. Instead of providing mutual protection and support in the struggle against temptation, they draw one another into sin. Instead of bearing one another's burdens, instead of leading one another to repentance and making a common confession of guilt, they accuse one another. "Again and again, man and woman abandon each other to solitude, and the two who are so intimately one can be more isolated from each other than enemies."[5]

Desire and *domination*, mutual lust and mastery, are inseparably interwoven. "And so arises the strange battle of the sexes, more bitter than any other warfare, for here hatred is woven deeply into desire, rejection into the closest intimacy."[6] Especially heavy is the yoke of woman, even where medicine, technology, and modern life have outwardly improved her situation in many respects. New and more subtle slaveries have replaced the old ones. It would

---

[5] Romano Guardini, *Der Anfang*, 105.
[6] Ibid., 107.

be a fatal mistake to think that the March of Progress will gradually break all yokes and bring liberation. Hope lies elsewhere: in the yoke itself, which God imposed on man and woman not just for punishment but for healing and salvation.

Augustine calls marriage a "remedium concupiscentiae" (a remedy for concupiscence). In an admittedly somewhat free interpretation, we can take that to mean that the first consequence of the primal sin is concupiscence, the "inclination to evil" (CCC 405). It manifests itself above all as passionate self-absorption, which very easily turns the other person into an object of possession. The yoke of marriage is a remedy against self-absorption. It *makes one aware* of the other person, makes one *take* the other person seriously, makes one *accept* the other person, and so opens up the self-enclosed heart to the other person. This applies in a special way to motherhood, to the gift of the child, which can lead the parents out of and beyond themselves.

What Eucharistic Prayer IV says is particularly true of marriage through all the centuries of human history: "In thy mercy thou didst help all men to seek thee and to find thee." In the blessing of the bride in the old liturgy (today Nuptial Blessing for form A in the English sacramentary), the Church says of marriage that it is "the only blessing that *was not forfeited either in punishment of original sin or under sentence of the flood*". But it takes patience and the power of grace to heal the deep wounds inflicted by original sin on the relationship of man and woman.

3. *A dour combat.* The name *protoevangelium* is given to the promises that God made when he uttered a curse over the serpent: "I will put enmity between you and the woman, and between your seed and her seed; he shall bruise your head, and you shall bruise his heel" (Gen 3:15).

Combat is promised, but so is victory. The doctrine of original sin makes us realize that our situation is dramatic: "The whole world is in the power of the evil one" (1 Jn 5:19). The Council uses clear and urgent words to describe the same reality:

> The whole of man's history has been the story of dour combat with the powers of evil, stretching, so our Lord tells us, from the very dawn of history until the last day. Finding himself in the midst of the battlefield man has to struggle to do what is right, and it is at great cost to himself, and aided by God's grace, that he succeeds in achieving his own inner integrity.[7]

Nowadays we have too often forgotten that human life is a battle, and that this also applies in a new way to Christian life. Saint Augustine wrote a treatise *De agone christiano* (on the Christian struggle). Not for nothing did the Church Fathers take over the pagan Greek doctrine of the cardinal virtues, because in prudence and justice, in fortitude, temperance, and self-discipline, they saw remedies against concupiscence, which continues to affect the baptized. Today, when the ravaging of human life is so great, especially in the former Communist countries but also in the rich West, it is essential to promote the *simple virtues* that slowly but surely can restore a truly *human* life.

[7] GS 37, 2; CCC 409.

We are once more in a situation like that of Paul, who in a pagan culture had to remind the new Christians of the elementary *human* virtues. They are the *humus* of humanity, the ground-soil of the *humanum*, upon which the life of the divine virtues, the truly *Christian* life, can be grown. "Whatever is true, whatever is honorable, whatever is just, whatever is pure, whatever is lovely, whatever is gracious, if there is any excellence, if there is anything worthy of praise, think about these things" (Phil 4:8; CCC 1803). True human progress will always involve the cultivation of this *humus* of authentic humanity, its preservation from erosion, and, where it has been ruined, its restoration through patience and the courage of hope.

This struggle is unending as long as there is a world. It is the *praeparatio Ecclesiae*, the gathering up of men in the cause of the good, in the cause of community. For only goodness unites; sin splits and separates. As Origen says, "where there are sins, there are also divisions, schisms, heresies, and disputes. Where there is virtue, however, there also are harmony and unity, from which arise the one heart and one soul of all believers."[8] It is *Christ* who is our hidden guide and teacher in this struggle, the *magister interior*, the inner teacher of our hearts, the light that enlightens every man (cf. Jn 1:9). This is how he gathers up his people, prepares the way for his Church.

PRAISED BE JESUS CHRIST!

---

[8] *Homiliae in Ezechielem* 9, 1; CCC 817.

Third Meditation
The Covenant with Noah

"Again and again", we say in Eucharistic Prayer IV, "thou didst offer covenants to men. . . ." God created the world for the sake of the covenant, for the sake of the Church. The breach of sin did not destroy God's plan; it only changed the way in which it was to be fulfilled. What sin shattered and scattered, God's covenants with men were to gather up anew. This "gathering movement" is the Church. She is *prepared for in the Old Covenant*, which in turn is prepared for in the covenant with Noah.

Our reflections on this *first and broadest covenant* are of particular importance in this day and age, when the significance of the non-Christian religions is being discussed so intensely. *Here* we find the basis of *the Christian view of the world's religions*, of their significance in the history of salvation. But there are also some points of reference here for "political theology". For example, in the light of divine revelation, what is the significance of mankind's struggle for political *unity*? What are the implications of the diversity of peoples, languages, and races? These weighty issues can be only briefly addressed here and then left to each person's reflections.

1. Our meditation on the *protoevangelium* shows again what has already clearly emerged: God heals the wounds of sin *through those very wounds*. The effort of work becomes a way of *atonement*, a remedy. God transforms the discomforts of pregnancy and the painful tensions in the relationship of man and woman into a "remedy against concupiscence", against the self-absorption that comes from original sin. The proneness to evil that comes from Original Sin, the "inclination to evil", becomes a testing ground in the struggle for the good (cf. CCC 1264).

In the *covenant with Noah* we encounter further dimensions of the damage caused by original sin and their transformation into ways of salvation.

"Now the earth was corrupt in God's sight, and the earth was filled with violence" (Gen 6:11). The Bible's description of the cascade of violence, from Cain's fratricide to Lamech's seventy-sevenfold blood revenge (cf. Gen 4), has lost none of its relevance. Violence and murder are more rampant than ever, from the war against the weakest, unborn children and helpless elderly people to the possibility of mankind's collective nuclear self-destruction.

Throughout the history of salvation, God's answer will be to *choose an individual, or a small number* of individuals, in order to bring salvation and blessing *to all*. Without the mystery of *substitution*, we cannot grasp the meaning of the Church. The election of the righteous Noah and his family becomes a type of the Church. The Fathers and the liturgy have given us a detailed exposition of the *ark* as an image of the Church. I shall now say something about this.

Noah is first and foremost the exemplar of *the righteous pagan*. The prophet Ezekiel presents him as such along with Job and the otherwise unmentioned Daniel (cf. Ezek 14:14; CCC 58). The Old Testament recognizes and honors such great figures from the "nations", the Gentiles—Melchizedek, the King of Salem, is one of them. They all belong to the *covenant with Noah*, which can be seen as, in a sense, *the realm of the religions of mankind*. By honoring these "holy heathen", the Church ascribes a certain validity to their worship and service of God.

The sacrifice that Noah offers on the altar he himself has built is pleasing to God. As a result God promises that the cosmic order will continue to exist: "While the earth remains, seedtime and harvest, cold and heat, summer and winter, day and night, shall not cease" (Gen 8:22). And God seals his covenant with mankind and all living things through the sign of the rainbow in the sky (cf. Gen 9:12–17). This bond between worship and the cosmic order implies that in the religions of mankind authentic acts of reverence for God (*religio*) are practiced to which God responds with his favor. The figure of Melchizedek is further impressive proof of this, as are the offerings and prayers of the Gentile Job. If the religion of the righteous heathen can attain the high dignity of being a type of Christ, it is because Christ and his grace are already at work in it in a hidden way. We are not talking here simplistically about an "equality" of all religions but about the *semina verbi*, "the seeds of the Word",[1] which can be found wherever men such as Noah, Melchizedek, or Job serve God justly and worship him faithfully. At the same time, we must add that the religions of the nations have to decide for or against Christ and that since the coming of Christ they have been in a new situation. "The times of ignorance" are over, says Paul (Acts 17:30). "Now [God] commands all men everywhere to repent, because he has fixed a day on which he will judge the world in righteousness by a man whom he has given assurance to all men by raising him from the dead" (Acts 17:30–31).

Since "the fullness of time" arrived, the religions have been in *crisis*, under judgment, and the laughter of the Athenians about the resurrection of the dead is already a sign of this judgment. "Dialogue with the religions" cannot disregard the fact that "the end of the ages has already come upon us" (LG 48,3). However true it may be that "the Catholic Church rejects nothing of what is true and holy in these religions",[2] the serious question remains as to how far the situation of the religions today is deeply defined by their Yes or No to Christ. This question is particularly pressing in relation to Islam, which, albeit under the influence of the sins and divisions of Christians, has uttered a resounding No to the divine Sonship, Cross, and Resurrection of Jesus.

All the more urgent, then, is our Lord's command to

[1] Vatican Council II, Decree on the Church's Missionary Activity, *Ad Gentes Divinitus* (December 7, 1965), no. 11 (hereafter abbreviated as AG).

[2] Vatican Council II, Declaration on the Relation of the Church to Non-Christian Religions, *Nostra aetate* (October 28, 1965), no. 2.

make all nations his disciples (cf. Mt 28:19). With all the
more ardor must the fire of the Holy Spirit burn in the
disciples of Jesus: "Caritas Christi urget nos" (the love
of Christ urges us on) (2 Cor 5:14).

2. There is a second theme connected with the covenant
with Noah: *the significance of the diversity of nations, languages, and races in the saving plan of God.* Is it not strange
that our Lord gave his apostles the task of making "disciples of all *nations*" (Mt 28:19)? It is not enough to interpret this as a synonym for "all men", though doubt-
less it means that as well. The Revelation of John calls
Christ the "King *of the Nations*" (Rev 15:3) and makes
this promise: "All *nations* shall come and worship thee"
(Rev 15:4). What does this mean for the Church, which
in her final perfection will be, and in a sense already is,
a multitude past counting "from every nation, from all
tribes and *peoples* and *tongues*" (Rev 7:9)? Does it mean
simply that the just will be saved as individuals from the
mass of the nations? Why, then, does it say that at the
Last Judgment "*all the nations*" will be gathered before
the Son of Man (Mt 25:32) and that in the heavenly
Jerusalem "*the nations* shall walk by his light" and carry
their treasures into the City of God (cf. Rev 21:24–26)?
What is the significance of *the nations* and their treasures
(their cultures, languages, experience) for the Church,
God's "gathering movement"?

The great "table of the nations" in Genesis 10 shows
that the many nations of the earth have a *common origin*,
that they really do form a *single* family. Yet the breach of
sin was to break up this unity. The Tower of Babel (in

Genesis 11) is seen as the attempt by fallen men to produce unity *by themselves*, to demonstrate and to increase their *own* power, without God and against God (cf. CCC 398). The scattering of mankind across the face of the earth, the confusion of tongues is *God's punishment* for the hybris of men.

But this means that human beings really cannot restore unity, cannot undo the divisions of languages and peoples, *by their own unaided powers*. When they try to, the result is a totalitarian state and the constant temptation to achieve world domination.[3] God's punishment is salutary. *No man is abandoned by God to his fallen nature.* The punishment of being scattered, the *diaspora* of the nations, is also *a way of being healed, the possibility of being made holy*. God's original plan to make mankind his family now makes use of the solidarity of peoples and languages, of nations and races, *to prepare for his Church*. Paul speaks of this in the Areopagus: "And he made from one every nation of men to live on all the face of the earth, having determined allotted periods and the boundaries of their habitation, that they should seek God, in the hope that they might feel after him and find him. Yet he is not far from each one of us" (Acts 17:26–27).

This is, of course, a provisional arrangement. No people, no culture, no language has been given a pledge that it will exist forever, no people, that is, apart from *the Chosen People*, whom God has chosen for his own possession. What gives the peoples, the nations, *their identity*?

---

[3] Cf. J. Ratzinger, *Die Einheit der Nationen* (Salzburg: Pustet, 1971), 20f.

Neither language nor culture nor territory on its own, however important each may be, defines the identity of a people. No, it is best to say that a *common destiny* and *common history* are the decisive factors. Sacred Scripture shows that we are dealing here with a more than merely empirical reality when it confides each of the nations to the protection of its own *angel* (cf. CCC 57) and when it speaks of the riches and treasures, the heritage, of the nations that are to be brought into the People of God (cf. Is 60:7–11; Haggai 2:7; Rev 21:24–26). The virtue of patriotism, the readiness to serve one's native land, the love of the culture and language of one's own people: all this is a *praeparatio Ecclesiae* and has a proper place in the Church (cf. CCC 2239; 2310).

But the nations have not only guardian angels but also their own demons. Nationalistic pride, contempt for the "barbarians", xenophobia, the deification of one's own power: our century has seen the demonism of godless nations in all its naked ugliness! We too easily forget that our countries, the countries of the old Christendom, have been "exorcised" for centuries. For many generations, as communities and in their individual members, they have taken the path of penance and conversion, of grace and sanctification. For decades, in the tombs of Egypt, Antony fought against the demons of a "culture of death". Think how much Christian living and dying it took to soak our countries with the spirit of the gospel by which we still live today! And consider the idolatrous worship of the state during this century: Is it not the return of the expelled demons to the swept and empty house, so that in the end it is worse than it was before, in the days of paganism (cf. Mt 12:44–45)?

The Church can never identify herself with *one* nation. She is not a national Church. And yet the unmistakable features of the Church can be discerned *within* the different nations. This is never more beautifully or luminously expressed than in *the saints*. Who could be more French than Thérèse, more English than Thomas More, more Spanish than Ignatius, more Italian than Catherine and Francis? And yet none of them is *just* a "national saint", and any attempt to misuse the saints in the cause of nationalism (as has happened, for example, in the case of Saint Joan of Arc) totally misses the point of their lives.

A people, a nation, finds its identity only when it finds Christ. He received the nations from the Father as his "heritage" (cf. Ps 2:8). When he comes to a people through evangelization ("Make disciples of *all* nations", Mt 28:19), he comes to "his own" (Jn 1:11). Long before the gospel is proclaimed, the Lord has already begun to prepare a people for himself. *His grace has already gone ahead of the messengers of the gospel.* An impressive testimony to this truth can be found in the vision in which our Lord says to the Apostle Paul at the beginning of his mission in Corinth: "Do not be afraid, but speak and do not be silent; for I am with you, and no man shall attack you to harm you; for *I have many people in this city*" (Acts 18:9–10).

PRAISED BE JESUS CHRIST!

Fourth Meditation
The Old Covenant

We are entering upon holy ground (cf. Ex 3:5). The question of the significance of Israel and the Old Covenant, of the Torah and the promises, for our understanding of the Church takes us to the heart, the center of the mystery of the Church. What is the significance of the Old Covenant for the Church? What does the Council mean when it says that the Church was "prepared *in marvellous fashion (mirabiliter)* in the history of the people of Israel and the Old Covenant"?[1] With the coming of Christ, is Israel's role over and done with? Or is it still in some mysterious way a *preparation* for the Church? Does it have a significance "only" in this *preparation* and not in its own right? These questions are in no way mere theological tomfoolery, academic shadowboxing. They are burning questions for Israel and for the Church, questions weighed down with the oppressive burden of history. The wounds of our century are too deep, the load of guilt too great, for these questions to be discussed at a tranquil, neutral distance.

The questions we have posed are even weightier here in Rome, where Peter and Paul, Jews in the Jewish community of Rome, did their work as apostles of the Lord. Paul

---

[1] LG 2; CCC 759.

wrote pages to Rome that deal with the mystery of Israel and the Church in a way that no one else has ever done. I am thinking of chapters 9 to 11 of his epistle "to all God's beloved in Rome, who are called to be saints", whose "faith is proclaimed in all the world" (Rom 1:7-8).

There is so much that could be said about the history of the Jews in Christianized Rome. There are shadows as well as light in this heavy-laden history. Take, for example, Pope Anacletus II, who descended from the Jewish Pierleoni family and has entered into history as just an anti-pope. In 1930 Gertrud von Le Fort devoted a whole novel to him. *The Pope from the Ghetto* is one of the most profound things ever written in this bloody century about the mystery of Israel and the Church. We should also mention Pope Pius XII and everything that much-maligned man did for the Jews. I can never go past the Great Synagogue without thinking of Israel Zolli, the Chief Rabbi of Rome. On Yom Kippur 1944, as he stood before the shrine of the Torah, Christ the Lord appeared to him and his wife, and at his baptism, out of gratitude to Pope Pacelli [Pius XII], took the baptismal name Eugenio. And how can we forget the memorable visit of the Holy Father to the same Great Synagogue on April 13, 1986? When we tread upon this holy ground, we are not just *touching* the mystery of Christ, Israel, and the Church; it *surrounds* us on all sides!

Let us begin our meditation with the passage in the Catechism that deals with the election of Israel: "In order to gather together scattered humanity God calls Abram from his country, his kindred, and his father's house [cf. Gen 12:1], and makes him Abraham, that is, "the father of a multitude of nations" [Gen 17:5]. 'In you all the nations of the earth shall be blessed' [Gen 12:3, LXX]" (CCC 59).

In the call of Abraham we see God's great plan at work: to gather together all mankind to be his family. Where *one man* fell to the ruin of all, *one man* is to become a blessing for all: "The people descended from Abraham would be the trustees of the promise made to the patriarchs, the chosen people, called to prepare for that day when God would gather all his children into the unity of the Church. They would be the root onto which the Gentiles would be grafted, once they came to believe" (CCC 60). Then, a couple of paragraphs later: "After the patriarchs, God formed Israel as his people by freeing them from slavery in Egypt. He established with them the covenant of Mount Sinai and, through Moses, gave them his law so that they would recognize him and serve him as the one living and true God, the provident Father and just judge, and so that they would look for the promised Savior" (CCC 62). And finally: "Israel is the priestly people of God, 'called by the name of the LORD' [Dt 28:10], and 'the first to hear the word of God' [*Roman Missal*, Intercessions, Good Friday], the people of 'elder brethren' in the faith of Abraham" (CCC 63).

In the draft of the Catechism, the so-called *Projet révisé*, which was sent to all the bishops for their assessment, the original text ran as follows: "Israel is *not a nation*, but the priestly people of God." There was a storm of protest about this sentence, especially from Israel! It was a total misunderstanding! The sentence was misinterpreted as a statement by the Catholic Church about the present-day state of Israel. It was thought we were denying that Israel is a nation, a state among the states. In reality, this is a clear, *positive* affirmation about the *election* of Israel. It is not just one people among many, one nation among many, but God's own Chosen People. Israel is not a people existing in its own right that God sought out among the other peoples and then blessed with special privileges. No, God himself is Israel's *Creator* (cf. Is 43:15). It is *he* who made it *his* people. It has its existence through *his* choice.

But there is the rub. Is Israel ethnically a people, a race? That can hardly be maintained, now any more than in antiquity (cf. Acts 2:5–11). What gives Israel its identity is its priestly vocation to bless and to be a blessing: "You shall be to me a kingdom of priests and a holy nation" (Ex 19:6). Israel is above all an "assembly of people" before God, a *qahal*—the very reality that the Septuagint translates as *ekklēsia, Church*. Of course, Israel is also a people in the sense of having a common family tree. They are the seed of Abraham, to this very day, but these descendants exist only because God himself *gave* them to Abraham, and because Abraham *believed*.

The very *fact* of Israel's existence, beginning with Isaac and Jacob, is permanent proof of the incomprehensible *faithfulness of God*. Such a small people could not have such durability from its own resources, from its own merely ethnic identity: "He has helped his servant Israel, in remembrance of his mercy, as he spoke to our fathers, to Abraham and to *his posterity for ever*" (Lk 1:54–55). This fidelity of God is not, of course, one-sided. It is in covenant with the faith and fidelity of Abraham: "[B]ecause you have done this, and have not withheld your son, your only son, I will indeed bless you, and I will multiply your descendants as the stars of heaven and as the sand which is on the seashore . . . and by your descendants shall all the nations of the earth bless themselves, because you have obeyed my voice" (Gen 22:16–18).

No infidelity on the part of Israel, no sin of the people, not even the misjudgment and rejection of Jesus the Messiah, can ever destroy God's fidelity to "Abraham and his posterity for ever". And so Paul writes to the Christian community in Rome: "[A]s regards election they are beloved for the sake of their forefathers. For the gifts and the call of God are irrevocable" (Rom 11:28–29). Twice Paul asks the question, and twice he gives the resounding reply: "I ask, then, has God rejected his people? By no means! . . . So I ask, have they stumbled so as to fall? By no means!" (Rom 11:1, 11).

What does this mean for the Church? It opens up the need for a change of outlook, in fact, a change of heart. The indelible impression left by the Shoah, the Holocaust, teaches the same lesson. It makes us realize that the deadly hatred of Israel is also, deep down, aimed at the Church, in fact at the God of Israel himself, the Father of our Lord Jesus Christ.

There is much that ought to be said here. Let me mention just three areas in which a change of outlook is necessary and indeed already, to some extent, taking place. The Catechism points the way forward.

1. We cannot find Christ when he is cut off from his roots. The Catechism shows this in its meditation on

the Solemnity of the Epiphany (cf. CCC 528). The Wise Men from the East (cf. Mt 2:1–12) represent the "Church taken from the Gentiles". They show the permanently valid way for the pagans to come to Christ, even in our own times.[2] The Catechism says:

> The magi's coming to Jerusalem in order to pay homage to the king of the Jews [cf. Mt 2:2] shows that they seek in Israel, in the messianic light of the star of David, the one who will be the king of the nations. Their coming means that pagans can discover Jesus and worship him as Son of God and Savior of the world only by turning toward the Jews and receiving from them the messianic promise as contained in the Old Testament. The Epiphany shows that "the full number of the nations" now takes its "place in the family of the patriarchs" [Leo the Great] and acquires *Israelitica dignitas* [Easter Vigil, Prayer after third reading] (CCC 528).

The first thing to be noted about this very dense text is this: the ancient promise, that the nations will come and worship God in Israel, on Mount Zion, is fulfilled. From the beginning, the mission of Jesus is shown to fulfill this promise. He fulfills it, not, of course, in the Temple, not on Mount Zion, but *in his very person*: "He has made . . . both one" (Eph 2:14). The pagan religions, the world's religions, "can play the role of the star that puts men on the path, that leads them to search for the kingdom of God. The star of the religions points toward Jerusalem; it is extinguished and relit in the Word of God, in the

---

[2] On what follows, see Joseph Cardinal Ratzinger, *Gospel, Catechesis, Catechism*, trans. Adrian Walker (San Francisco: Ignatius Press, 1997), 73–96.

Holy Scripture of Israel. The Word of God preserved in Scripture appears as the true star, which we cannot dispense with or ignore if we wish to reach the goal."[3]

What does this mean? It means that the Gentiles, the nations and religions of the world, can only find Christ, and so can only become *Church*, when they enter into the promises of Israel, when the history of Israel becomes *their* history. "Salvation is from the Jews" (Jn 4:22). There is no access to Jesus, and therefore no entry to the People of God, without the acceptance by faith of the revelation of God that speaks to us in the Sacred Scriptures of the Old Testament.

The Old Testament is and will always be God's great catechesis in preparation for Christ. That is why the Old Testament cannot and must not be replaced by the writings of other religions. We must not try to solve the difficulties of the Old Testament by removing its readings from the liturgy but by learning to read and love and expound it in the light of Christ. A Carthusian lay brother once said to me: "The Old Testament is the love story of God."[4]

2. The second point concerns this very question of the correct way of reading the Old Testament, in other words, the question of the relationship of the Old and New Testaments. The Catechism regards *typology* as a privileged expression of their unity. We are talking here, not about *one* exegetical method among *many*, but about a deeply

[3] Ibid., 77.

[4] Cf. J. M. Garrigues, *Ce Dieu qui passe par les hommes: Conférences de Carême* II (Paris, 1993), 98f.

theological view of salvation history. Typology is not a method of interpreting *texts* but a distinctive view of the *events* of salvation history. It derives from the fact that God's saving plan is *one*. The events of the Old Testament foreshadow the events of the New Testament; they are "prefigurations of what [God] accomplished in the fullness of time in the person of his incarnate Son" (CCC 128). Just as the ark saved Noah and his family, so even more does baptism save us now (cf. 1 Pet 3:21).

This does not devalue the Old Testament, as the Catechism insists time and again: "The calling of the patriarchs and the exodus from Egypt, for example, [do not] lose their own value in God's plan, from the mere fact that they were intermediate stages" (CCC 130). No, "typology indicates the dynamic movement toward the fulfillment of the divine plan" (ibid.). But this also means that the Church can never renounce the Old Testament. To do so would be to disown *God himself*, for he is the God of Abraham, Isaac, and Jacob, a God of *the living*, not of the dead (cf. Mk 12:26–27).

3. One sore point is the relationship of law and gospel. If the Church is *wonderfully* prepared for in the Old Testament, in what sense does *the law* prepare for *the gospel*? By contrast to the widespread contemporary view that law and gospel are in opposition to each other, the Catechism sees them in a relationship of promise and fulfillment: "The Lord's Sermon on the Mount, far from abolishing or devaluing the moral prescriptions of the Old Law, releases their hidden potential and has new demands arise from them: it reveals their entire divine and human truth.

It does not add new external precepts, but proceeds to reform the heart, the root of human acts" (CCC 1968).

At this point, in line with the Catechism, which stands in the great Catholic tradition, we need to consider and *reflect* on why and how Jesus perfectly fulfills the law. The Jewish tradition has its own feast of "*rejoicing in the Torah*". One takes the Torah under one's arm, as if it were a bride, and dances with it in the synagogue.[5] The reason why joy in the law of God is so great is that it springs from his very own will, from his heart. According to a Jewish tradition, it is the *Torah* that is *the beginning* in which God created heaven and earth. It is the plan of God's heart, the plan by which he created the world, the plan that he revealed to his people. That is why there is no greater happiness than being totally faithful to God's law. Jesus will even say that this fidelity is *his* "*food*" (Jn 4:34).

This is all just a hint, a sketch. We can grasp the heart of the matter if we go back to what we said earlier: the mysterious encounter of Israel Zolli with Jesus Christ in the Great Synagogue in Rome. It took place when the Rabbi was standing in front of the *shrine of the Torah*. Is not Christ "the fulfillment of the law"? Is he not "the beginning" in whom, through whom, for whom God created all things, and in whom God's plan is carried out: the Church?

Opposite the Great Synagogue of Rome, in Lungotevere dei Pierleoni, stands a small church, San Gregorio. Above the entrance is an inscription in Hebrew and Latin. It calls the Jews to conversion. *Here*, for centuries (from

---

[5] Cf. Bella Chagall, *Brennende Lichter* (Hamburg: Rowohlt 1966).

the time of Pius V to Pius IX), *sermons* were given to which the Jews were obliged to listen. Is it not now a time of conversion for us? This church, at the entrance to the ghetto, bears witness to the long history of suffering of God's beloved Chosen People. The Council said that *the Church* is "wonderfully prepared" (*mirabiliter praeparata*) in the Old Testament and in the history of the people of Israel. Perhaps today we realize more deeply that this remains valid, through the permanent presence of the people of Israel, until the Lord himself returns to perfect the Church.

PRAISED BE JESUS CHRIST!

THE CHURCH—
INSTITUTED IN THE LAST DAYS

First Meditation
"And the Word Was Made Flesh"

"But when the time had fully come, God sent forth his Son, born of a woman, born under the law, to redeem those who were under the law, so that we might receive adoption as sons" [Gal 4:4–5]. This is "the gospel of Jesus Christ, the Son of God" [Mk 1:1]: God has visited his people. He has fulfilled the promise made to Abraham and his descendants. He acted far beyond all expectation —he has sent his own "beloved Son" [Mk 1:11; cf. Lk 1:55, 68] (CCC 422).

With these words the Catechism begins its chapter on Jesus Christ.

If it is true that "the mystery of man becomes clear only in the mystery of the Word made flesh" (GS 22), then how much more so does the mystery of the Church! All her light comes from Christ. The very first sentence of the Council's Dogmatic Constitution on the Church begins with that certainty: "*Lumen Gentium cum sit Christus*. . . . Since Christ is the light of the nations; it is the heartfelt desire of this Sacred Council, which has been gathered together in the Holy Spirit, to shed on all men that radiance of his *which shines upon the face of the Church*. This it will do by proclaiming the Gospel to every creature (LG 1)". Christ is the center. He is the Sun of Righteousness. To use a favorite comparison of the Fathers, the Church only has *his* light, just as the moon can only reflect back the light of the sun.[1] This is her condition in the time of her pilgrimage: she longs to abide with Christ the Sun (*permanere cum Sole*),[2] to leave behind all the cares of her wayfaring state.

When we look at the situation of the Church today, we have to face the urgent question: Has the first sentence of *Lumen Gentium* become enough of a reality? Do we honestly and truly look at the Church in the light of Christ and in relation to him? Do we see the Church as having her *very being in him*? Is there not too much talk about the Church? Has the Church not been too preoccupied with herself? Cardinal Ratzinger presented this diagnosis at the Extraordinary Synod in 1985.[3] The more the Church turns her face to Christ, the more she will radiate his light, and the more she will shine with her proper beauty.

There is another phenomenon that is a cause for concern. Christ is more and more often conspicuously absent from ecclesiastical talk. There are whole pastoral programs, with game plans and models of action and guidelines, that do not mention the name of Christ even

---

[1] Cf. Hugo Rahner, "Mysterium Lunae", in *Symbole der Kirche* (Salzburg: Muller, 1964), 91–173.

[2] Cf. Augustine's commentary on Ps 71:5.

[3] *Synode extraordinaire: Célébration de Vatican II* (Paris: Cerf, 1986), 428–30.

once. Some people openly insist that there should be less
talk about Christ and more about God, so that what separates us from the other monotheistic religions is not too
evident. The way was paved for this trend over many
years by the insidious undermining of faith in the true
divinity of Christ and thus of faith in the true Incarnation of the Son of God. But whatever the *Church* is in her
innermost essence, she receives entirely from Christ. We
can approach the mystery of the Church only through
the door of Christmas. But the converse is also true: we
can find our way to the Crib, to the "tent of God among
men", only with our fellow travellers in the community
of faith: As Saint Cyprian says, "no one can have God as
Father who does not have the Church as Mother" (CCC
181).

In fact, Christ and the Church are one. The Catechism
quotes the wonderfully simple and clear answer of Saint
Joan of Arc to the suggestion of her theologian-judges
that perhaps she was faithful to Christ but not to the
Church: "About Jesus Christ and the Church, I simply
know *they're just one thing*, and we shouldn't complicate
the matter" (CCC 795). Today's meditations will, therefore, be devoted to Christ and the Church.

Let us return to the text quoted at the beginning, the
text with which the Catechism introduces its confession
of faith in Christ: "[W]hen the time had fully come, *God
sent forth his Son*, born of a woman, born under the law,
to redeem those who were under the law, so that we
might receive adoption as sons" (Gal 4:4-5). In this central confession of Saint Paul's faith in Christ, we find the
elements for today's four meditations:

1. "God sent forth his Son, born of a woman." The mystery of the Incarnation is our first theme.

2. The mission of the Son is meant to bestow *sonship* upon us. The second meditation considers the concrete form of that sonship: the mysteries of Jesus.

3. The mission of Jesus is ordered toward a "we", a community, the Church. We shall look at the "Super hanc petram" (on this rock) text (Mt 16:18) in relation to this foundation of the *ekklēsia* as a community.

4. Finally, we shall deal with the "ransoming" of those who are under the law, the mystery of redemption. The theme will be *Ecclesia ex latere Christi*, the birth of the Church "from the side of Christ".

On major feasts in many of the churches of my homeland, including Saint Stephen's Cathedral in Vienna, so-called "orchestral Masses" are played and sung. There is not a single one of these Masses, whether by Mozart or Haydn, Schubert or Bruckner, where the "Et incarnatus est" of the Creed is not especially heartfelt and tender. It is as if the music itself wanted to *kneel down* and *adore*: *Venite adoremus!* Now, as we approach the Jubilee of the Incarnation, our thoughts and prayers should also *kneel down* and *adore* the mystery of Christmas. Perhaps it will be possible, on the occasion of the Jubilee Year, to reintroduce back into the Creed, at the "Et incarnatus est", the general practice of genuflection. There is a lovely "short

text" in the Catechism (CCC 563) from one of the spir-
itual masters of our century, though here he is unnamed:
"No one, whether shepherd or wise man, can approach
God here below except by kneeling before the manger at
Bethlehem and adoring him hidden in the weakness of a
new-born child."[4]

The first thing that must adore and kneel down is *the
intellect*, in union with the will, with the whole heart. That
is a lot to ask of the intellect! Some years ago a group of
English theologians argued as follows: The God-manhood
of Jesus is incompatible both with God's being God and
man's being man.[5] We are dealing here, they said, with
mythological talk, and such talk does not claim to state
real historical truths. So talk about the Virginal Concep-
tion of Jesus is mythological, as is talk about the empty
tomb and the real bodiliness of the Risen Lord. But how,
then, can the Church be real as a mystery both divine
and human?

A few years after Easter, Christians sing a hymn—Paul
gives it to us in his letter to the Philippians—in which
Christ is worshipped as pre-existent in the form of God
and as obedient unto death, and, like us, in the form of a
servant. But that is not all. We are also told explicitly that
all creatures in heaven and on earth and under the earth
bend the knee and worship him—all this in words that in

[4] See Fr. Marie-Eugène, O.C.D., *I Want to See God: A Practical Synthesis of Carmelite Spirituality*, trans. Sr. M. Verda Clare, C.S.C. (Notre
Dame: Fides, 1953), 78. [The translation given in the Catechism dif-
fers slightly from Sr. Verda Clare's—TRANS.]

[5] Cf. J. Hick, ed., *The Myth of God Incarnate*, 2d. ed. (London: SCM
Press, 1993).

the Old Testament, in Isaiah (cf. 45:23), expressly refer to *God*. This is the *great* scandal, the stumbling stone for believing Jews, as it is also for Moslems. The Dominican exegete Father François Dreyfus, who is of Jewish descent, writes of it as follows: "One needs to have experienced the spiritual journey of Saint Paul to gauge the *enormous* difficulty that faith in the Incarnation represents for an orthodox Jew. . . . Only in retrospect, in the light of faith, does one discover that the Trinity and the Incarnation do not contradict the monotheistic dogma of Israel."[6]

"Believe in God, believe also in me" (Jn 14:1). What kind of man can say such a thing about himself, except by some delusion of *hybris*? What kind of man can say of his teachings, "Heaven and earth will pass away, but my words will not pass away" (Mt 24:35)? Faced with our Lord's holiness, Peter recognizes himself as a sinner and falls down on his knees in worship (cf. Lk 5:8). The man born blind falls down before him and confesses his faith (cf. Jn 9:38). The very name the disciples give him also expresses adoration: *the Lord* (CCC 446–51). Faith in the one God, the Father, and faith in the one Lord, Jesus Christ, are inseparable (cf. 1 Cor 8:6). "Belief in the true Incarnation of the Son of God is the distinctive sign of Christian faith" (CCC 463). Only in adoring faith can the searching intellect receive the light in which the mystery of the Incarnation begins to shine and be clear. Then it attains its wonderful luminous power, lighting

---

[6] *Jésus savait-il qu'il était Dieu?* 2d. ed. (Paris: Éditions du Cerf, 1984), 63.

up all things human and divine: the mystery of man and the mystery of the Church.

Two texts of the Council in a special way unfold the "divine-human" constitution of the Church. The first is in the second article of the Constitution on the Liturgy. We are told there that in the liturgy the mystery of Christ is expressed, as is the essence of the true Church:

> The Church is essentially both human and divine, visible but endowed with invisible realities, zealous in action and dedicated to contemplation, present in the world, but as a pilgrim, so constituted that in her the human is directed toward and subordinated to the divine, the visible to the invisible, action to contemplation, and this present world to that city yet to come, the object of our quest.[7]

The second text is of the utmost importance. It is one of the core statements of Vatican II about the mystery of the Church. With four pairs of concepts, this subtly articulated text outlines the parameters of the *one* Church of "the one Mediator Christ". The holy Church is at one and the same time both "*community* of faith, hope, and charity" and the "*visible organization*" that Christ established and ever sustains here on earth. She is both a "society structured with hierarchical organs" and the "Mystical Body of Christ", both a "visible society" and a "spiritual community". And she is, finally, both "the earthly Church" and "the Church endowed with heavenly riches". Then comes the conclusion: these pairs are "not to be considered as two different quantities, but

[7] Vatican Council II, Constitution on the Sacred Liturgy, *Sacrosanctum concilium*, no. 2 (hereafter abbreviated as SC); CCC 771.

rather form one complex reality which comes together from a human and a divine element".[8] The Council goes on to say very carefully: "*By an excellent analogy*, the Church is compared to the mystery of the incarnate Word. Just as the assumed nature, inseparably united to the divine Word, serves him as a *living instrument of salvation*, so in a very similar way the social structure of the Church serves the Spirit of Christ, who vivifies it, for the building up of the Body" (LG 8).

According to an image often used by the Fathers and Saint Thomas, the humanity of Christ is the "living salvific instrument" of the divinity of Christ. During the early centuries of the Church, in the long struggle for the right confession of faith in Christ, the councils affirmed that "in Christ human nature was assumed without being absorbed" (GS 22,2). The humanity of Christ is not a passive instrument. Christ has a human soul, intellect, and will. He has *a human heart*: "He has loved us all with a human heart" (CCC 478).

There is an analogy to this in the Church. She is not a passive instrument but a "social structure" animated by the Holy Spirit, with all the human gifts of her members, with all the human cooperation of individuals and communities, yet in such a way that they "serve the Spirit of Christ . . . for the building up of the Body" (LG 8,1). "Without ceasing", Christ sustains the Church, precisely as *this visible structure*. However, in a way that is different from Christ himself, the Church *must grow up* toward him. She must "follow constantly the path of penance and re-

[8] LG 8; CCC 771.

newal" (LG 8,3). He is perfect, but "she [still] walks on her pilgrim way amidst the world's persecutions and God's consolations",[9] and yet she bears within herself, as his beloved Bride, all his glory. "Nigra sum sed formosa", black am I but comely, ye daughters of Jerusalem (Song 1:5). Saint Bernard expounds this text as follows:

> O humility! O sublimity! Both tabernacle of cedar and sanctuary of God; earthly dwelling and celestial palace; house of clay and royal hall; body of death and temple of light; and at last both object of scorn to the proud and bride of Christ! She is black but beautiful, O daughters of Jerusalem. . . . If you are repelled by her blackness, be amazed by her beauty."[10]

Whatever the Bride is, she owes totally to the Bridegroom. Her mystery is grounded in his. But the door to his mystery is *Christmas*: "Et Verbum caro factum est". If we worship this mystery without tiring, a sense of the mystery of the Church grows within us. *Genuflecting* at "Et incarnatus est de Spiritu Sancto ex Maria Virgine et homo factus est" could help us to do that.

PRAISED BE JESUS CHRIST!

---

[9] Augustine, quoted in LG 8, 4.
[10] St. Bernard of Clairvaux, *In Canticum sermones* 27:14; CCC 771.

Third Day

Second Meditation
The Mysteries of the Life of Jesus

In *Catechesi tradendae* are these words: "At the heart of catechesis we find, in essence, a Person, the Person of Jesus of Nazareth, the only Son from the Father. . . . [To catechize is] to reveal in the Person of Christ the whole of God's eternal design reaching fulfillment in that Person."[1] But this is still *external*. Catechesis is not just a question of *knowledge* about Jesus, of how we *describe* him, but a participation in his life, living communion with him. That is why *Catechesi tradendae* goes on to say: Catechesis aims at putting "people . . . in [*living*] *communion* . . . with Jesus Christ; only he can lead us to the love of the Father in the Spirit and make us *share in the life of the Holy Trinity*."[2]

The Church's meaning and goal is this *living communion* with the triune God. The question, therefore, of whether Jesus instituted and willed the Church is not *primarily* answered by being able, as it were, to cite "acts of institution" and adduce a historical process of foundation. The historical question of the Church's foundation is important—we should not try to evade it. However,

[1] CT 5; CCC 426
[2] Ibid.

what has *priority* is the question of *how* Christ communicates his life, how he gives men a share in his life: that is Jesus' real "foundation of the Church".

To answer this question, we must refer, once again, to the mystery of the *Incarnation*. In the Pastoral Constitution *Gaudium et spes*, we find this sentence, which the Holy Father often quotes. It is a key proposition, of immense importance: "By his Incarnation he, the Son of God, has in a certain way united himself with each man."[3]

The Incarnation of the eternal Son is his most fundamental communication of life to mankind. This does not take place, of course, in a kind of automatic process, as feared by many critics of this common patristic view. But what does this "communication of life" by Christ involve? What is the "communion of life" that *Catechesi tradendae* calls the goal of catechesis? The Second Epistle of Peter speaks of our "becoming partakers of the divine nature" (2 Pet 1:4), and following this the Church Fathers speak of the *divinization* of man. The Catechism (cf. 460) sums up this doctrine with the words of Saints Irenaeus, Athanasius, and Thomas Aquinas: "For this is why the Word became man, and the Son of God became the Son of Man: so that man, by entering into communion with the Word and thus receiving divine sonship, might become a son of God" (Irenaeus). "For the Word of God became man so that we might become God" (Athanasius). "The only-begotten Son of God, wanting

[3] GS 22, 2; CCC 521.

to make us sharers in his divinity, assumed our nature, so that he, made man, might make men gods" (Thomas Aquinas).

But what does it actually mean to speak about "making men divine"? There is no question, of course, of our humanity being "swallowed up" in God. Jesus *is* true God *and* true man. Saint Maximus the Confessor tells us that when man is made divine, "divinized", his *humanity* is not altered, but the *manner* of his being human is *renewed*. The humanity of Jesus is "divinized", not by the abolition of his humanity, but by his *new way* of being human: he alone, in all he does and says and *is*, is *Son*. His humanity is radically "filial", not "servile".

In *Gaudium et spes*, following the text quoted above, the Council gave a classical exposition of our Lord's *new way of being human*: "With human hands he [the Son of God] worked, with a human mind he thought, with a human will he acted, and *with a human heart he loved*" (GS 22,2). The Son of God loved with a human heart. He imprinted his eternal filial love on his human heart. *As man*, he is "the beloved Son" of the eternal Father. It is a share in the life of the triune God that we receive when we are given the grace to participate in Jesus' way of *being human*. We are given a place at the very heart of the Blessed Trinity when we receive a participation in Christ's Sonship, when we become sons-in-the-Son. It was for this end that we received "the Spirit of [God's] Son into our hearts", the Spirit who cries "Abba! Father!" (Gal 4:6).

Becoming the Church means, then, at the deepest level, receiving a participation in the Sonship of Jesus. "Make our hearts like unto thy Heart"—that prayer asks God to give us a "filial" heart, a Son-like heart. "Conform our life to thine"—that is how we can pray when we ask for the growth of the Church. Becoming the Church means that "Christ [is] formed in you" (Gal 4:19).

But how is this to take place? Through our participation in *the mysteries of the life of Jesus*. As is well known, the Catechism presents the life of Jesus, not in the style of a historico-critical reconstruction, but in the perspective of the "mysteries of the life of Jesus". This is how not only the Church Fathers but also the spiritual masters of the modern age, from Saint Ignatius Loyola, through the French School, to Dom Columba Marmion, read and interpreted the life of Jesus. It is also the way the liturgy recommends that we look at the life of Jesus. On the Solemnities of the Lord, whenever we celebrate the events of the life of Jesus, we celebrate also our *participation* in those mysteries. The life of Jesus is meant to become ours, he in us and we in him.

The Catechism lists the basic qualities that are common to the mysteries of Jesus and some ways in which we can participate in them. First, what do we mean by the "mysteries of Jesus"? A definite way of looking at the life of Jesus: he is true God and true man. Whoever looks at his life with this faith sees in it everywhere "the traces of his innermost mystery".

> From the swaddling clothes of his birth to the vinegar of his Passion and the shroud of his Resurrection, everything in Jesus' life was a sign of his mystery. . . . His humanity appeared as "sacrament," that is, the sign and instrument, of his divinity and of the salvation he brings: what was

visible in his earthly life leads to the invisible mystery of his divine sonship and redemptive mission (CCC 515).

"The mysteries of the life of Jesus"—those words mean that our Lord's whole life is the *sacramentum salutis*. The Catechism unfolds three characteristics of this "sacramentality" of the life of Jesus.

1. "Christ's whole earthly life—his words and deeds, his silences and sufferings, indeed his manner of being and speaking—is *Revelation* of the Father" (CCC 516). That is why it is so important *to contemplate* the life of Jesus *meticulously*, to let oneself be "impregnated" by its smallest details, by its every scene, by the gestures and words of Jesus. In this way, everything in the life of Jesus becomes the fulfillment of his words: "He who has seen me has seen the Father" (Jn 14:9). This, of course, presupposes that we confidently confess with the Council: "Our Holy Mother, the Church . . . firmly holds that the Four Gospels, *whose historicity she unhesitatingly affirms, faithfully hand on what Jesus, the Son of God, while he lived among men, really did and taught for their eternal salvation, until the day when he was taken up.*"[4] Only if this is true can we practice in meditation the "application of the senses" and "composition of place" recommended by Saint Ignatius in the *Exercises*.[5] It has been rightly pointed out that this vigorous meditation on scenes from the life of Jesus, which gives full play to the senses, has been a con-

---

[4] Vatican Council II, Dogmatic Constitution on Divine Revelation *Dei verbum* (November 18, 1965), no. 19.

[5] No. 47.

stant and fruitful inspiration for Christian art, which has never tired (until our "critical" century) of venerating and contemplating the life of Jesus.[6] The deep mistrust of the historical reliability of the Gospels that has grown over the last two hundred years impedes this living contemplation. On the other hand, historical criticism has enormously enriched, and made more vivid, our *knowledge* of Jesus' time and place and of the Jewish roots of his words and deeds. Might one not say that today, through historical criticism, *our Lord* has become for us more alive, more personally present, and, dare I add, more incarnate?

2. "Christ's whole life is a mystery of *redemption*. Redemption comes to us above all through the blood of his cross, but this mystery is at work throughout Christ's entire life" (CCC 517). His poverty, his obedience, his hunger and thirst, his tears over his friend Lazarus, his nights of prayer, his compassion for men—*everything* in his life has redemptive power. That is why communion with his life is redemptive and healing. That is why he heals through the Church.

3. "Christ's whole life is a mystery of recapitulation. All Jesus did, said, and suffered had for its aim restoring fallen man to his original vocation" (CCC 518). Saint Thomas unfolded this idea through his doctrine of the *gratia capitis*, the grace of headship. In all that Christ is and does, *he* is the head of the new humanity: "He is the Head of the body, the Church" (Col 1:18). Here we are already

---

[6] Cf. A. Besançon, *L'Image interdite: Une Histoire intellectuelle de l'iconoclasme* (Paris: Fayard, 1994), 246–48.

touching on the further explanations of the Catechism. How does *Jesus'* life become *ours*? How can we share in it? In his encyclical *Redemptor Hominis*, the Holy Father says that all Christ's riches "are for every individual and are everybody's property."[7] The Catechism mentions three ways in which Christ wants to make his life ours: by living his life *for us, before us, and in us.*

a. "Christ did not live his life for himself but *for us*, from his Incarnation 'for us men and for our salvation' to his death 'for our sins' (1 Cor 15:3) and Resurrection 'for our justification' (Rom 4:25). He is still our advocate with the Father' (1 Jn 2:1), who 'always lives to make intercession' for us (Heb 7:25)" (CCC 519). The only foundation of this "pro-existence" of Christ (to use a phrase of Professor Heinz Schürmann's) is *his love*. In his "Prayer of a Soul Taken with Love", Saint John of the Cross is not exaggerating when he draws this conclusion from the fact of the *pro me*: "Mine are the heavens and mine is the earth. Mine are the nations, the just are mine, and mine the sinners. The angels are mine, and the Mother of God, and all things are mine, and God Himself is mine and for me, because Christ is mine and all for me."[8]

---

[7] John Paul II, encyclical *Redemptor Hominis* (March 4, 1979), no. 11; CCC 519.

[8] "Sayings of Light and Love", in *The Collected Works of St. John of the Cross*, trans. Kieran Kavanaugh, O.C.D. and Otilio Rodriguez, O.C.D. (Washington, D.C.: Institute of Carmelite Studies, 1979), 669. The Spanish original is as follows: "*Míos son los cielos y mía la tierra, míos son las gentes, los justos son míos y míos los pecadores, los ángeles son míos y la Madre de Dios y todas las cosas son mías, y el mismo Dios es mío y para mí, porque Cristo es mío y todo para mí.*"

This is not the expression of some individualistic piety but the very foundation of the Church: *Christ—our life.*

b. "In all of his life Jesus presents himself as *our model*" (CCC 520). Incarnation means the *perceptibility* of salvation: salvation can be handled, heard, and seen in the living, suffering, and dying of Jesus. That is why the *practical* imitation of Christ is always part of the Church's life. It is also why the Church always needs *the saints*, in whom Christ becomes "seeable". In the *imitatio Christi* we attain a share in his life: "I have given you an example, that you also should do as I have done to you" (Jn 13:15). If there is to be harmony between the outward and the inward, Christ's life must become *wholly* our own:

c. "Christ enables us *to live in him* all that he himself lived, and *he lives it in us*. . . . We are called only to become one with him, for he enables us as the members of his Body to share in what he lived *for us* in his flesh as our model" (CCC 521). In what follows the Catechism begins to unfold this vision of the mysteries of the hidden and public life of Jesus (CCC 522–667). In fact, one might say that the whole of the rest of the Catechism is an unfolding of this way of looking at the life of our Lord. So, for example, the Church's liturgy and Sacraments are the living continuation of what Jesus did for us "once for all" (Heb 10:10): "The mysteries of Christ's life are the foundations of what he would henceforth dispense in the sacraments, through the ministers of his Church, for 'what was visible in our Savior has passed over into his mysteries' [Pope St. Leo the Great]" (CCC 1115). The Catechism's third part, in its very title ("Life in Christ"), also shows us the perspective in which Christian moral-ity is seen. Saint John Eudes gives concrete expression to the words of Saint John of the Cross: If Christ is wholly mine, then *his* Heart is *mine*, as are *his* spirit, *his* body, *his* soul, all *his* faculties. I must use them *for* him, *with* him. As we read the moral part of the Catechism, this perspective must not be overlooked:

> I ask you to consider that our Lord Jesus Christ is your true head, and that you are one of his members. He belongs to you as the head belongs to its members; all that is his is yours: his spirit, his heart, his body and soul, and all his faculties. You must make use of all these as of your own, to serve, praise, love, and glorify God. You belong to him, as members belong to their head. And so he longs for you to use all that is in you, as if it were his own, for the service and glory of the Father [Saint John Eudes] (CCC 1698).

PRAISED BE JESUS CHRIST!

Third Meditation
"And on This Rock. . . ."

The Church is inseparably two things: a *spiritual communion* and a *visible structure*, duly constituted here on earth. The visible structure, which is at the same time the spiritual communion, has a *concrete history*, which in turn has a clearly defined prehistory. "The Lord Jesus inaugurated his Church by preaching the Good News, that is, the coming of the Reign of God, promised over the ages in the scriptures."[1] "The seed and beginning of the Kingdom are the 'little flock' of those whom Jesus came to gather around him, the flock whose shepherd he is. They form Jesus' true family" (CCC 764).

Jesus himself gives this community a rule of life, a certain order, a task to be accomplished. *He himself* is, without doubt, the center of this community: *his* words, *his* instructions, above all *his person*. What no rabbi ever claimed for himself, Jesus makes the starting point of his community: "Follow *me*" (Mk 1:17; 2:14). In the circle of the disciples of the rabbis, the Torah stood at the center; here it is Jesus. The students of the Torah seek out a teacher and master for themselves, but here another rule applies: "You did not choose me, but I chose you

---

[1] LG 5; CCC 763.

and appointed you that you should go and bear fruit"
(Jn 15:16). Jesus himself teaches his "family", his circle
of disciples, a new way of living and acting (cf. Mt 5–
6). He gives them their own new prayer, the Our Father
(cf. Lk 11:2–4).

When Jesus speaks of his task of gathering together
the lost sheep of the House of Israel (cf. Mt 15:24), of
his mission of seeking out "the lost sheep" (cf. Lk 15:4–
7), he uses parables and images, which all contain a kind
of "implicit ecclesiology": for example, the image of the
wedding banquet, of God's sowing of the seed, of the
fisherman's net (cf. Mk 2:19; Mt 13:24, 47). What Jesus
announces in images and parables already has its real beginning in the community he gathers around him. The
Catechism says: "The Lord Jesus endowed his community with *a structure* that will remain until the Kingdom
is fully achieved. Before all else there is the choice of
the Twelve with Peter as their head. Representing the
twelve tribes of Israel, they are the foundation stones of
the new Jerusalem" (CCC 765).

Does this mean that the Church is built on the hierarchy? Is she not rather a *communion of life* with Christ?
What is the role of "structure"? The Catechism addresses
the issue thus:

> In the Church this communion of men with God, in the
> "love [that] never ends" [1 Cor 13:8], *is the purpose* which
> governs everything in her that is a sacramental *means*, tied
> to this passing world [cf. LG 48]. "[The Church's] struc-
> ture is totally ordered to the holiness of Christ's members.
> And holiness is measured according to the 'great mystery'
> in which the Bride responds with the gift of love to the

gift of the Bridegroom."[2] *Mary* goes before us all in the
holiness that is the Church's mystery as "the bride without
spot or wrinkle" [Eph 5:27]. This is why the "Marian"
dimension of the Church precedes the "Petrine" [cf. MD
27] (CCC 773).

This is a helpful distinction. Like the whole of the sacramental and institutional structure of the Church, the hierarchy is part of the *order of means* in the Church. The only
goal of all these means is and should be *the holiness* "that
is the Church's mystery". That is why *Mary* is the living
embodiment of what the Church in her *essence* is. This
also explains the important but often misunderstood *essential distinction* between the common priesthood and the
hierarchical priesthood (cf. LG 10). The common priesthood belongs to the order of the goal: the new life in
Christ, regeneration by water and the Holy Spirit. The
ministerial priesthood is one of the means toward that
end that our Lord has given his Church. The task of the
ordained ministry in the Church is to be a sacrament of
Jesus Christ and, therefore, a means and instrument, a
"servant of Jesus Christ". Just as the Church as a whole
is called a "living instrument of salvation" (in LG 8), so
those whom Christ has called to his service are meant to
be his *living* instruments.

With sovereign freedom ("[He] called to him those
whom he desired", Mk 3:13), Jesus chooses and calls a specific group of men to follow him. He "*makes* them to be
the Twelve" (cf. Mk 3:14), deploying his *creative power*,

[2] John Paul II, apostolic letter *Mulieris dignitatem* (August 15, 1988),
no. 27 (hereafter abbreviated as MD).

the power by which he is the Creator of Israel, indeed, the Creator of the world. Their vocation is not to serve Christ in some neutral way but to be drawn ever more deeply into a total communion of destiny with him. Mark tells us that Jesus called them and made them the Twelve so that they might *be "with him"* (Mk 3:14). *Here* they begin to grow into the *two* dimensions of their future apostolic ministry: they are the Church as *communion with Christ*, but at the same time they are *commissioned men*, men with a mission, sent in the power of Christ, "to be with him, and to be *sent out* to preach and have authority to cast out demons" (Mk 3:14). Their apostolic ministry is entirely sustained by this *"being with Christ"*. This, too, will be his promise at the end, in Galilee, at the beginning of their worldwide mission: "And lo, *I am with you* always, to the close of the age" (Mt 28:20).

The way of the disciples who become the apostles is, then, a way walked with Jesus. They walk with him, and they exist with him. This has two *inseparable* aspects: a *visible office* with authority and a task to be accomplished and, at the same time, distinct yet never to be separated from it, a *spiritual communion* with Christ through faith, hope, and love. Thus the mystery of the Church is reflected in her ordained ministry.

It is a constant cause of surprise and wonder to see the honesty and truthfulness with which the Gospels report the fact that the disciples were not "star pupils" in the school of the Master. Is it not one of the strongest arguments for the historical credibility of the Gospels that they should give such a candid and unvarnished record of the apostles' shortcomings and failure to understand?

And what a mirror of pastoral ministry for *us*, who are their successors! To go from "*being with Jesus*" at the beginning to "*being in Christ*" as described by Saint Paul is a long journey.

Jesus' "school of discipleship", what we might call his *scuola di communità*, provides inexhaustible material for meditation. I should like to make some suggestions for our own meditations today. It is especially the Evangelist Mark who records the "obstinacy" of the disciples. This is seen above all in their *lack of faith, their lack of* "amor pastoralis", *and their bickering over rank and dignity*. The temptations of pastors have remained the same to this day.

1. Let us take the scene in Mark 6:30–44 as a first example. Jesus invites the disciples to go to a lonely place with him and to rest a while. The crowd finds out and hurries on ahead. "As he landed he saw a great throng, and he had compassion on them, because they *were like sheep without a shepherd*" (Mk 6:34). Our Lord's shepherdly love attracts the crowds. His shepherdly Heart is preoccupied, not with his own rest, but with the sheep without a shepherd. By contrast, this is what we are told about the disciples: "When it grew late, his disciples came to him and said, 'This is a lonely place, and the hour is now late; *send them away*, to go into the country and villages round about and buy themselves something to eat" (Mk 6:35–36). *Send the people away!* What kind of pastoral concern for their fellow men is it when all they care about is their own rest, when they are fearful of complications? Even when there is a genuine pastoral concern,

it has not been trained in the school of Jesus: "You give them something to eat" (6:37). These two texts should be painful to us: "Send the people away—*You* give them something to eat!" They are the elements of our examination of conscience. The very spontaneity of this reaction of the apostles shows us clearly how little the thinking of Christ has up to this point shaped their own thinking and striving.

2. In another scene the roles appear to be reversed. Jesus seems harsh and unpitying, while the disciples seem full of kindness. Jesus is in the Gentile district of Tyre and Sidon. A Gentile woman comes and cries out: "Have mercy on me, O Lord, Son of David; my daughter is severely possessed by a demon. But he did not answer her a word" (Mt 15:21–23). Jesus seems harsh and cold. The disciples are different: "[They] came and begged him, saying, 'Send her away, for she is crying after us'" (15:23). They beg Jesus to help the poor woman. Needless to say, their real motive is betrayed by the words, "she is crying *after us.*" It is awkward *for them*, this scene of a crying woman, who will not give them any peace—and in a foreign, heathen country at that! Our Lord's behavior seems to become even harsher. Without looking at the woman, he says: "I was sent only to the lost sheep of the house of Israel" (Mt 15:24). Awkward or not, this woman is not in his "field of competence". Again Jesus' harshness seems to reach a crescendo: "But she came and knelt before him, saying, 'Lord, help me.' And he answered, 'It is not fair to take the children's bread and throw it to the dogs'" (15:25–26). It gets no harsher than this: the woman is turned away as

a "Gentile dog". But here comes the breakthrough, the turning point. "Yes, Lord," says the Canaanite woman, "yet even the dogs eat the crumbs that fall from their master's table" (15:27). "Then Jesus answered her, '*O woman, great is your faith!* Be it done for you as you desire.' And her daughter was healed instantly" (15:28). Jesus' behavior was only apparently harsh. From the first moment, he had perceived the woman's great heart, her readiness to believe. His remote manner provoked the courage of her faith. How magnificent it is when God, the Son of God, himself cries out in amazement at the faith of a human being: "O woman, great is your faith!" Outwardly Jesus *seems* cold, but in reality he is on the alert for this encounter. *Sitit sitiri*, he thirsts to be thirsted for (cf. CCC 2561). He thirsts for her faith, as he does when he meets the Samaritan woman. Meanwhile, the disciples are trapped in the stupidity of their self-concern. What a "confessional mirror" this holds up before us! It challenges and tests our "compassion". Is it just "Anything for a Quiet Life"? Or "Avoid Complications"? Or "We Don't Want a Public Outcry"? Or "No Awkward Scenes, Please"? Is there a thirst for the *salvation* of men burning in our hearts, a thirst for their *faith*, for the enlarging of their hearts by testing? How does our *amor pastoralis* shape up in the mirror of this Gospel scene?

3. A short scene, again a real "confessional mirror": "And they were bringing children to him, that he might touch them; and the disciples rebuked them. But when Jesus saw it, he was indignant, and said to them, 'Let the children come to me, do not hinder them'; . . . And he took

them in his arms and blessed them, laying his hands upon them" (Mk 10:13–16). The Evangelist does not tell us *why* the disciples abused and barked at the people. Were they trying to protect Jesus, to get these tiresome people off his back? Or did they feel it would be undignified to bring children to the Master? After all, children had no understanding of his words, his teaching . . . What is important is the very fact *that* the Evangelist gives us this simple and honest report, which includes Jesus' anger with his disciples. Again, some words, a scene, that can be a mirror for our confessions: "Do not hinder them", let them come to me! Three scenes that show us what we know, or should know, only too well: how often it is we, the apostles and their successors, who hinder people from coming to Jesus!

There are two further scenes that we must look at briefly. They lead us more deeply into *the drama of the sin of the shepherds*, which is already so painfully familiar to us from the Old Testament.

4. It is just after our Lord's Transfiguration. He has told the disciples for the second time that he will have to suffer and be killed, but that on the third day he will rise again. "And they came to Capernaum; and when he was in the house he asked them, 'What were you discussing on the way?' But they were silent; for on the way they had discussed with one another who was the greatest" (Mk 9:33–34). He foretells his Passion, but they are talking about precedence and promotion. It is hard to grasp how their hearts could have been so dulled. No one asks *him*, no one *comforts him*, in the face of his coming death—that would have been the simple reaction of the heart. No,

the Evangelist says: "They did not understand the saying, and they were afraid to ask him" (Mk 9:32). Again, all credit to the evangelists for preserving this honest picture of the disciples. And yet how shocking is their silence before Jesus, as they leave him all alone, and how shocking their talk on the road, where everything revolves around them! How can they be so oblivious of his suffering? And how great is his love for them, whom he chose *to be with him*, these men whose hearts and minds are so often so far from him!

5. There is one scene in the Gospels that gives us a sense of how far this love goes. It is played out in, so to speak, the Holy of Holies. "I have earnestly desired to eat this passover with you before I suffer" (Lk 22:15). On this incomparable evening, when our Lord gives us his testament for us to do in remembrance of him until he comes again, on this evening when he washes the disciples' feet and hands them his Body and his Blood, the greatest gift of his love, "*a dispute* arose among them, *which of them was to be regarded as the greatest*" (Lk 22:24). And yet, at this moment, no scolding words come from Jesus. Instead, he says, "The kings of the Gentiles exercise lordship over them; and those in authority over them are called benefactors. But not so with you; rather let the greatest among you become as the youngest, and the leader as one who serves. For which is the greater, one who sits at table, or one who serves? Is it not the one who sits at table? But I am among you as one who serves" (Lk 22:25–27).

The Lord is "the one who serves", even his uncomprehending, sceptical (cf. Mk 4:40), hard-hearted (cf. Mk 6:52; 8:17) disciples. He does not condemn them. *He* does *not* send them away. He lets them come to him. And in *this* hour of all hours, after *this* shameful scene, he says one of his most powerful words, which should be considered as the solemn institution of the apostles' ministry: "You are those who have continued with me in my trials." Oh, it wasn't very glorious, this "continuing" by the apostles, but our Lord knows that they had and have the *will* to do it, despite all their failures. "*As my Father appointed a kingdom for me, so do I appoint for you*, that you may eat and drink at my table in my kingdom, and sit on thrones judging the twelve tribes of Israel" (Lk 22:28–30). Now, in the very hour when all the apostles desert *him*, *our Lord* empowers their ministry. And now, too, Simon Peter receives the promise that, thanks to our Lord's prayer for him, *his faith will not fail* (cf. Lk 22:31). "Super hanc petram aedificabo Ecclesiam meam" (Mt 16:18). The Rock is, first of all, *the belief* that Jesus is the Christ, the Son of the living God (cf. CCC 424). The Rock is Christ himself. Only in his strength and by his word is Peter also the Rock.

The apostolic ministry is the means ordained by Christ for attaining the Church's goal. The unworthiness of the minister cannot "prevent Christ from acting" (CCC 1584). And yet it is precisely *this unfathomable humility of our Lord*, who is willing to use *us* for building up his Church, that should shake our sluggish hearts and move us to tears of repentance (cf. Lk 22:61–62): "Lord, you know everything; you know that I love you" (Jn 21:17).

PRAISED BE JESUS CHRIST!

Fourth Meditation
The Church Born from the Side of Christ

The whole earthly life of Jesus is "foundational" of the Church in the broad sense that we have outlined in the three previous meditations today. Now we need to go one step farther in the company of the Catechism:

> The Church is born primarily of Christ's total self-giving for our salvation, anticipated in the institution of the Eucharist and fulfilled on the cross. "The origin and growth of the Church are symbolized by the blood and water which flowed from the open side of the crucified Jesus" [LG 3]. "For it was from the side of Christ as he slept the sleep of death upon the cross that there came forth the 'wondrous sacrament of the whole Church'" [SC 5]. As Eve was formed from the sleeping Adam's side, so the Church was born from the pierced heart of Christ hanging dead on the cross (CCC 766).

Here the Council takes up a common theme of the Church Fathers. The Church owes everything to the self-giving of Christ on the Cross. *Here* is her source of life and renewal. From this source flow the sacraments of the Church. This source is present in the Eucharist, which is why the Eucharist is called "the source and summit of the Christian life".[1]

[1] LG 11; CCC 1324.

The Church owes everything to the Cross. What does this mean for her being, for her course through history, for us as servants of the Church? The Cross of Jesus is a historical event, not a "natural necessity". It is an event willed, procured, and carried out by men. At the same time it took place "according to the definite plan and foreknowledge of God" (Acts 2:23). The Cross stands at the intersection between the historical actions of men and the saving plan of God. It is one of the most horrific instruments of torture ever devised by man's imagination, but at the same time we greet it as our "only hope": "Ave Crux, spes unica." The arms of Jesus, dislocated and stretched out on the Cross, are a terrible sight, and yet these far-extended arms both symbolize and effect what Jesus promised: "And I, when I am lifted up from the earth, will draw all men to myself" (Jn 12:32).

In terms of her origin in the Cross, the Church has two characteristics: she bears with Christ the shame of the Cross, and, through Christ, she is a sign of hope. But there is a tremendous difference between the two: Christ alone bears the reproach of the Cross without blame. The Cross of the Church is always the shame of her sinful members. That is why it is *his* Cross that is our *spes unica*. That also is why, as the Catechism explains, we do not say that we "believe *in* the Church, so as not to confuse God with his works and to attribute clearly to God's goodness *all* the gifts he has bestowed on his Church" (CCC 750). And it is for this very reason that *our only hope is in the Cross of Jesus Christ*: we *all* need the gift of atonement.

Our *meditatio crucis* must first ask how the death of our

Lord on the Cross came about. This will show that truly sober historical research does *not* take us away from the mystery of faith but runs into it. Historical exegesis has made the reasons for the death of Jesus in many respects much clearer.

1. How did the death of Jesus come about?

One thing is clear from the testimony of the Gospels. The real reason for the condemnation of Jesus was strictly religious. His conduct was felt to be blasphemous precisely because it revealed that he was acting with God's own authority. "You, being a man, make yourself God" (Jn 10:33; cf. 5:18). As the conflicts with the religious authorities in Jerusalem show, the deepest point of dispute was the question of our Lord's authority, ultimately of his identity (cf. especially Mk 12). How could a mere *man* say, "He who loves father or mother *more* than *me* is not worthy of *me*; and he who loves son or daughter more than *me* is not worthy of *me*" (Mt 10:37)? Is not the Fourth Commandment the *first* commandment of love of *neighbor*? The implication is that *this* demand made by Jesus belongs to the love of *God*, to the first three commandments. How could a mere *man* dare to say, "Every one who acknowledges *me* before men, the Son of man also will acknowledge before the angels of God" (Lk 12:8)? How is the *eternal* salvation of man supposed to depend on his attitude to *Jesus*?

We sense how outrageous these and other words, deeds, and gestures must have seemed to the religious leaders. It was becoming more and more clear that the moment of decision was approaching. The man who was "for Jesus" also accepted his words and acknowledged that he came from God. And so the Scribes and Pharisees believed that they had to reject Jesus in the name of God himself. Their No to Jesus was intended to be an act of fidelity to God. But if they rejected Jesus, how were they to explain his good deeds, his healings, and the powers within him never before seen or heard? "No man ever spoke like this man!" (Jn 7:46). In this dramatic conflict the religious leaders thought they were "offering service to God" (Jn 16:2) by having Jesus killed. Did the death of Jesus *have* to take place? Is it like a Greek tragedy, where, with a kind of inevitability, everything converges in catastrophe? Could it have turned out differently?

Did Jesus not woo Israel with all the love and passion of his Heart? Did he not do everything to move his people to conversion? The earnestness of our Lord's endeavor can be seen in his shattering tears of lamentation over Jerusalem. As he approached the city, in the place where the pilgrims broke into jubilation at the sight of the city and the Temple (cf. Ps 121), Jesus weeps and says: "Would that even today you knew the things that make for peace! But now they are hid from your eyes" (Lk 19:42). And then there is the other great lamentation of Jesus, the lamentation of God over "his first love": "O Jerusalem, Jerusalem, killing the prophets and stoning those who are sent to you! *How often would I have gathered your children together* as a hen gathers her brood under her wings, *and you would not!*" (Lk 13:34).

So is the unbelief of the Jews to blame for the death of Jesus? They did "not know the time of your visitation"

(Lk 19:44). "And you would not. . . ." Jesus summed up the situation in a little parable: "To what then shall I compare the men of this generation, and what are they like? They are like children sitting in the market place and calling to one another, 'We piped to you, and you did not dance; we wailed, and you did not weep'" (Lk 7:31–32). Where does this refusal come from, this attitude of *"we will not"*, "we will not play"? When he was crucified, Jesus prayed: "Father, forgive them; for they know not what they do" (Lk 23:34). Does this apply directly only to those who crucified him? Peter himself after Pentecost says: "Brethren, I know that you acted in ignorance, as did also your rulers" (Acts 3:17). Paul confirms, "If they had [known], they would not have crucified the Lord of glory" (1 Cor 2:8).

"Ignorant": Does that mean the same thing as "innocent"? There is, of course, a real story of guilt in the Crucifixion of Jesus. It begins with the hardness of heart of those who object to our Lord's healings (cf. Mk 3:1–6): here people really *will* not see and will not hear. Then there are the disciples' flight and betrayal, the calculating politics of the Temple aristocracy, the cowardice of the Roman governor, the faint-heartedness of the members of the Council. But behind this narrower circle of individual failures, omissions, and betrayals, the sum total of which led to the death sentence against Jesus, we can see *outer circles of complicity*: all of Israel's guilt in the past. For generation after generation ("*How often* would I have gathered your children together. . . .") Israel has said her No to God: "And you would *not*."

But is it only Israel's history of guilt that here strikes

against the Innocent? *Further* circles of guilt and sin emerge, circle after circle, all stemming ultimately from that first and most momentous *No*, the No of Adam's sin. Every No ever directed toward God is concentrated in the hour of our Lord's rejection. For in this hour the whole Yes of God is at stake. Can there be a greater sin than the rejection of Jesus, with whom God has given us everything (cf. Rom 8:32)? But that is not all: sin, every sin, is at its core a rejection of Jesus, the Son of God, the eternal Word, through whom all things were created and to whom all things belong: "He came to *his own home*, and his own people received him not" (Jn 1:11).

The Crucifixion of Jesus is the action of individual men at a specific time, the time when Pontius Pilate was governor of Judea. And yet this action of theirs is not something isolated and detached. Behind their action are *all* sins of all times, for every sin is No to God's "right of ownership". Like the first sin, *every* sin is the act of not believing in him. Those who rejected him did not *believe* in him, and so they crucified him. To the question of the cause of the Passion of Jesus, the Roman Catechism answered that, in addition to original sin, the cause of the Passion was *all* the sins and vices that have ever been committed by men from the beginning of the world to its final consummation.[2] Only the Holy Spirit can open up *this* dimension of the Cross, to which merely historical observers of the events are blind. Of the Spirit, Jesus says that he will convince the world of sin, and this sin is that "*they do not believe in [him]*" (Jn 16:8‒9).

[2] 1, 5, 11; CCC 598.

We crucified Jesus. This shattering realization came to the Apostle Paul the day he encountered the Risen Lord. Jesus was crucified *because of my sins*. Paul was given this understanding at the very moment he was overwhelmed by the realization: "Jesus died *for my sins*". This shocking truth that Paul was responsible for the Crucifixion of Jesus only became a certainty for him in the light of the truth that he presents in the letter to the Galatians as the summing up of his conversion: "The Son of God loved *me* and gave himself up *for me*" (Gal 2:20).

2. "He died for our sins in fulfillment of the Scriptures"

We saw that the question of responsibility for the death of Jesus can be fully addressed only when we recognize in faith *the One who* was given up for us on the Cross. How could the Son of God be killed by his own creatures? "He came to his own home, and *his own people* received him not." We have a sense that *this* rejection is not a distressing accident in the history of the world, which is dense with such injustices. *The rejection of Jesus is the accumulation of everything that ever was, is, or will be sin. Yes, what sin really is, its real gravity, becomes visible only on the Cross: at the infinite cost he paid to heal us.*

In his famous dialogue *Cur Deus homo*, Saint Anselm of Canterbury says to his disciple Boso: "Nondum considerasti quanti ponderis sit peccatum" (You have not yet realized how great is the weight of sin).[3] It is hard for us even to make guesses about this weight. On the Cross

---

[3] *Cur Deus homo* 1, 21.

the Son of God smote the "sin of the world", and only through the Cross is sin revealed in its core as the refusal to allow God his right of ownership, as therefore the denial of the truth about ourselves ("everything is *his*"), and so ultimately as the rejection of God. *And it is precisely this Cross that is transformed by God into an instrument of salvation.*

In the parable of the wicked tenants of the vineyard, the logic of the story demands that the monstrously iniquitous murder of the son and heir should be repaid with draconic punishment: "What will the owner of the vineyard do? He will come and destroy the tenants, and give the vineyard to others" (Mk 12:9). That would be the obvious *solution* to the guilt of the tenants. We deserve that solution. But instead, something unimaginable takes place: God himself transforms the rejection of his Son by sinners into the forgiveness of their sins. What happens is not *the resolution [Lösung] of guilt through merited punishment but the redemption [Erlösung] of the guilt itself.* Instead of the tenants being condemned to punishment and executed for their wicked deed, the Owner of the vineyard does the unthinkable: he delivers up his Son into their hands. Their wicked deed brings about his good deed. The Son dies *by* the hands of his murderers, yet the Father gave him into their hands, so that he might die *for* them.

In his speech at Pentecost in Jerusalem, Peter says: "This Jesus, delivered up according to the definite plan and foreknowledge of God, you crucified and killed by the hands of lawless men. But God raised him up" (Acts 2:23–24). Here, in its highest measure, the mystery of Providence is enacted. The very thing that is the wicked deed of men turns out to be—by the good and incomprehensible will of God—*his* good deed for us. Once again the "analogy of faith" comes to our aid. At the end of the story of Joseph and his brothers, Joseph says to them, once they have realized the wrong they have done him: "As for you, you meant evil against me; but God meant it for good, to bring it about that many people should be kept alive, as they are today" (Gen 50:20). The Catechism adds: "From the greatest moral evil ever committed—the rejection and murder of God's only Son, caused by the sins of all men—God, by his grace that 'abounded all the more', brought the greatest of goods: the glorification of Christ and our redemption. But for all that, evil never becomes a good" (CCC 312).

3. Redeemed by the Cross of Jesus

On the Cross Jesus overcame all of mankind's No to God by his great and incomparable cry of Yes: "It is finished" (Jn 19:30). Every No to God, the sin of the world, brought him to the Cross. On the Cross Jesus overcame the No. In Gethsemane Jesus fully accepted the will of the Father, let himself be delivered up for us, and with all his human will said Yes to the Father ("Not my will, but thine. . . ."). For all of us, he said the liberating Yes to the Father. "*In him we have redemption*" (Col 1:14). He is both God's Yes to us and man's Yes to God. Redemption means, therefore: *him* for *me*, him in my place. "He loved *me* and gave himself up *for me*." Again let us think of the parable in Mk 12: the evil tenants killed the last messenger, the son. We killed the "Lord of Glory", but this did not become condemnation for us: he let himself be struck down by us and be given up for us. *Before* anything we can do, and more encompassing than anything we may fail to do, is this "for us" of Christ.

An enigma, of course, remains unresolved: there is this *prevenient gift* of "for us", but is there something or someone "against us"—death, the devil, or we ourselves? "What shall separate us from the love of Christ?" (Rom 8:35), asks Paul. He says he is sure that *nothing* can separate us from Christ. Nothing? Not even my own No? My own "I will not"? Is there not a danger of my locking myself in a final and definitive No? What are we praying for in the Roman Canon when we say, "Deliver us from eternal damnation"? Why do we pray silently before receiving Holy Communion, "Deliver me by this thy most sacred Body and Blood from all mine iniquities and from every evil . . . and *suffer me never to be separated from thee*." Every time he said those words, the Curé of Ars is said to have wept . . .

PRAISED BE JESUS CHRIST!

THE CHURCH—REVEALED BY THE OUTPOURING OF THE HOLY SPIRIT

First Meditation
"He Gave Up His Spirit"

"When the work which the Father gave the Son to do on earth was accomplished (cf. Jn 17:4), the Holy Spirit was sent *on the day of Pentecost* in order that he might continually sanctify the Church" [LG 4]. Then "the Church was openly displayed (*manifestata*) to the crowds and the spread of the Gospel among the nations, through preaching, was begun" [AG 4]. As the "convocation" of all men for salvation, the Church in her very nature is missionary, sent by Christ to all the nations to make disciples of them (CCC 767).

Have we been overlooking the Holy Spirit? We have been talking about creation, about the Old Covenant, and about Christ—without explicitly mentioning the Holy Spirit. Is that just my neglectfulness? Is it a sign that the Holy Spirit is often overlooked, often forgotten? Is it perhaps like the situation in Ephesus when Paul met some disciples who had to confess quite openly: "We have never even heard that there is a Holy Spirit" (Acts 19:2). But perhaps this "forgetfulness" has another cause. Could it be that somehow it is typical of the Holy Spirit?

In the third chapter of the first part of the Catechism, the chapter on the Holy Spirit, we read as follows:

"No one comprehends the thoughts of God except the Spirit of God" [1 Cor 2:11]. Now God's Spirit, who reveals God, makes known to us Christ, God's Word, his living Utterance, *but the Spirit does not speak of himself.* The Spirit who has "spoken through the prophets" makes us hear the Father's Word, *but we do not hear the Spirit himself.* We know him only in the movement by which he reveals the Word to us and disposes us to welcome him in faith. The Spirit of truth who "unveils" Christ to us "will not speak on his own" [Jn 16:13]. *Such properly divine self-effacement* explains why "the world cannot receive [him], because it neither sees him nor knows him," while those who believe in Christ know the Spirit because he dwells with them [Jn 14:17] (CCC 687).

The Holy Spirit precedes faith, awakens it, directs and guides it. And yet in the order of revelation the Spirit is "the last of the persons of the Holy Trinity to be revealed" (CCC 684). The goal of catechesis is to put "people . . . in communion . . . with Jesus Christ" (CCC 426). And that is precisely the goal *of the Church*: total living communion with Christ. "[T]o be in touch with Christ, we must first have been touched by the Holy Spirit" (CCC 683).

How does this happen? *How* does the Holy Spirit *touch* us? *How does he reveal Christ*? If he does not touch and teach the heart from within, then the best methods of proclamation are useless. The Acts of the Apostles show how the spreading of the gospel was directed by the Holy

Spirit, how he opens the door to the gospel—or even closes it (cf. Acts 16:6, 8, 14).

From the beginning the Spirit is at work, inseparably from the Word, who was "in the beginning", and the Spirit was God, just as the Word was God (cf. Jn 1:1). And just as the Word, the Logos, carries out everything in creation and the Covenants, so does the Holy Spirit. *In the Catechism* we find an entire catechesis on the *hidden working* of the Holy Spirit from the creation "until 'the fullness of time' [Gal 4:4]" (CCC 702). This catechesis should help us to read the Old Testament in terms of "what the Spirit, 'who has spoken through the prophets,' wants to tell us about Christ" (CCC 702). Here the Catechism tries, albeit in brief outline, to lead us to an exegesis as desired by the Council. In *Dei verbum* 12, 3—an extremely important text—it says: "Sacred Scripture must be read and interpreted in the light of the same Spirit by whom it was written" (CCC 111). "[U]ntil 'the fullness of time' [Gal 4:4], the joint mission of the Father's Word and Spirit remains *hidden*, but it is at work. God's Spirit prepares for the time of the Messiah. Neither is fully revealed, but both are already promised, to be watched for and welcomed at their manifestation" (CCC 702).

The catechesis on the Holy Spirit in the Old Testament does not use *allegorical exegesis* but instead reads the concrete events and stages of the Old Covenant, from the creation to John the Baptist (CCC 703–720), as the patient preparation for Christ. The Spirit, the hidden "Giver of Life", is everywhere, already at work and yet still unknown, indeed, still not "given": "For as yet the Spirit

had not been given, because Jesus was not yet glorified"
(Jn 7:39). Those words of John's Gospel come from a
passage that was much commented on by the Fathers.[1]

> On the last day of the feast, the great day, Jesus stood up
> and proclaimed, "If anyone thirst, let him come to me,
> and drink. He who believes in me, as the scripture has
> said, 'Out of his heart shall flow rivers of living water.'"
> Now this he said about the Spirit, which those who be-
> lieved in him were to receive; for as yet the Spirit had not
> been given, because Jesus was not yet glorified (Jn 7:37–
> 39).

> [I]n these "end times", ushered in by the Son's redeem-
> ing Incarnation, the Spirit is *revealed* and *given*, *recognized*
> and *welcomed* as a person. Now can this divine plan, ac-
> complished in Christ, the firstborn and head of the new
> creation, be embodied in mankind by the outpouring of
> the Spirit: as the Church (CCC 686).

Pentecost is certainly the moment when the Church is
made manifest, but the Holy Spirit is first *given on the Cross*:
"For as yet the Spirit had not been given, because Jesus
was not yet glorified" (Jn 7:39). Now Jesus' glorification
took place *on the Cross*. It is here, in his love "to the end"
(Jn 13:1), that the Spirit is given. Here, in *this* hour, "the
work of our redemption is accomplished." That is why
we turn again to the *mystery of the Cross* in order to develop the meditation we began yesterday on the birth of

---

[1] Cf. Hugo Rahner, "*Flumina de ventre Christi*. Die patristische Ausle-
gung von Joh. 7,37.38", in *Symbole der Kirche* (Salzburg, 1964), 177–
235.

the Church "from the side of Christ" (*ex latere Christi*) by reflecting on the *giving of the Holy Spirit* in the hour of Jesus' glorification. For the Cross, the Paschal Mystery, remains the source from which the Church receives and pours forth the "streams of living water", the Holy Spirit.

We considered yesterday how the condemnation and killing of our Lord was both the wicked action of man and the saving action of God. This interweaving of the human act of sin and the divine act of grace is expressed by a linguistic peculiarity in the New Testament. The word "hand over" or "give up" (*paradidonai, tradere*) is used for both the saving act of God and the wicked act of man. So we hear, for example, that Judas "betrayed", or "handed" Jesus over (*tradidit illum*, Mt 10:4 and parallels), or that Jesus is "delivered" into the hands of sinners (for example, Mk 9:31; Lk 24:7). Yet the same word is also used for God's saving decree: in the passive form, "he *was* given up for our trespasses" (Rom 4:25), or by allusion to Abraham's sacrifice: "[God] did not spare his own Son but *gave him up for us all*" (Rom 8:32). Paul also says several times that Christ "gave *himself* up"—*for him*, Paul (cf. Gal 2:20), *for us* (cf. Eph 5:2), *for the Church* (cf. Eph 5:25). And again the same word is used when our Lord says: "*All things* have been *delivered* to me by my Father" (Mt 11:27).

As he looks at the Cross, which is both the act of the sinner and the saving act of God, Paul asks: "Will he not also give us *all* things with him?" (Rom 8:32). This "*all*" is the Father's beloved Son himself. In his encyclical on the Holy Spirit, *Dominum et vivificantem*, the Holy Father writes:

> Already the "giving" of the Son, the gift of the Son, expresses the most profound essence of God, who, as Love, is the inexhaustible source of the giving of gifts. The *gift made by the Son* completes the revelation and giving of the eternal love: the Holy Spirit, who in the inscrutable depths of the divinity is a Person-Gift, through the work of the Son, that is to say, by means of the Paschal Mystery, is given to the Apostles and to the Church in a new way, and through them is given to humanity and the whole world.[2]

In order to reconcile us to himself, the Father gave up his own Son, his eternal Word, who—to use the wonderful phrase of Saint Thomas Aquinas—is "Verbum spirans Amorem" (the Word breathing out Love). Out of love for us, the Son "handed himself over" to the Father, and out of love for the Father, he gave himself up for us: " 'Father, into thy hands I commit my spirit.' And having said this, he breathed his last" (Lk 23:46). John says: "And he gave up his spirit [*tradidit spiritum*]" (Jn 19:30). The "spirit" referred to here—according to modern exegesis and the dominant interpretation of the Fathers—is the soul, the human spirit of Jesus. But the event is open to *the Holy Spirit* whom Jesus promised and who is now *given*. On the Cross, the Son gives *everything*, his whole life. In his dying as man, he is the "Verbum spirans Amorem". On the Cross the Blessed Trinity is revealed. The Father has

---

[2] John Paul II, encyclical *Dominum et vivificantem*, (May 18, 1986), no. 23, (hereafter abbreviated DEV).

given us his *all*, his Son. The Son has given us his *all*, his life. Both bestow *the Gift, the Love, in person*: the Holy Spirit.

This would all be just a dream had Christ remained in death. But *he is risen!* He was "raised from the dead by the glory of the Father" (Rom 6:4). The first gift of the Risen Lord is the Holy Spirit. But before our Lord breathes on the disciples and says, "Receive the Holy Spirit" (Jn 20:22), he shows them his hands and side (cf. Jn 20:20). The Holy Father speaks of this in his encyclical:

> He gives them this Spirit, as it were, *through the wounds* of his Crucifixion. . . . It is in the power of this Crucifixion that he says to them, "Receive the Holy Spirit." Thus there is established *a close link between the sending of the Son and the sending of the Holy Spirit. There is no sending of the Holy Spirit* (after original sin) *without the Cross and Resurrection.* . . . The mission of the Son, in a certain sense, finds its "fulfillment" in the Redemption. The mission of the Holy Spirit "draws from" the Redemption. . . . The Redemption is *totally carried out* by the Son . . . offering himself finally in sacrifice on the wood of the Cross. And this Redemption is, at the same time, constantly being carried out in human hearts and minds—in the history of the world—by the Holy Spirit, who is the "other Counsellor" (DEV 24).

Here we return to the starting point of our meditation. On the day of Pentecost, the Holy Spirit began the "manifestation" of the Church, the "time of the Church", her outward and inward, visible and spiritual growth. But the Holy Spirit was *given* on the Cross, and this source re-

mains the wellspring of the Church. The pierced Heart of
the Redeemer is the source of infinite love, from which
the Holy Spirit pours forth upon us (cf. CCC 478).

"The time of the Church" is, therefore, not a different time from the time of the crucified and risen Lord,
who sends us the Spirit from the Father. The time of
the Church is the time of the Holy Spirit, whom Christ
breathed out on the Cross and on the evening of Easter
Sunday. There will, therefore, be no "New Age", no
other times than these "last times" in which we have
been existing ever since the first Easter. And the Holy
Spirit leads us nowhere other than to him, from whom
he takes in order to give to us (cf. Jn 16:14): the Spirit
leads us *to Christ*.

The Church is the place where "the Spirit flowers".[3] As
Saint Irenaeus says: "It is in her that *communion with Christ*
has been deposited, that is to say: *the Holy Spirit. . . .* For
where the Church is, there also is God's Spirit; where
God's Spirit is, there is the Church and every grace"
(CCC 797). How do we recognize him, the Spirit of
Truth and Love? How do we distinguish his activity from
the activity of other spirits, good and evil? "The world",
says Jesus, "cannot receive [him], because it neither sees
him nor knows him" (Jn 14:17). Nothing is more necessary in our pastoral ministry than this *gift of discernment*. It
will help us avoid "quenching the Spirit" (cf. 1 Th 5:19)
and enable us to be "led by the Spirit" (cf. Rom 8:14;
Gal 5:18). Only then will we be free, the sons of God,

---

[3] "Locus ubi Spiritus Sanctus floret" (St. Hippolytus, *Traditio apos-
tolica* 35; CCC 749).

truly the Church, in other words, the family of God. And only then will we find the happiness for which we long and which can only be given by the Holy Spirit, the *dulcis hospes animae* (the soul's sweet Guest).

PRAISED BE JESUS CHRIST!

Second Meditation
"Look upon the Faith of Thy Church!"

The Church, according to the Council, is "the community of faith, hope, and charity".[1] Among all the statements about the mystery of the Church, this one stands
in first place. Today we consider the "manifestation"
of the Church through the Holy Spirit. We could apply
ourselves to the many aspects of this theme that concern
the *public* manifestation of the Church. For example, the
First Vatican Council mentions the Church's "marvellous propagation, eminent holiness, and inexhaustible
fruitfulness in everything good, her Catholic unity and
invincible stability", all of which, taken together, constitute "a great and perpetual motive of credibility and an
irrefutable witness of her divine mission".[2] However, in
the general perspective of these exercises, we should consider not so much these outward signs as the Church's
inward principle of life.

The "soul" of the Church is the Holy Spirit. "To
this Spirit of Christ, as an invisible principle, is to be
ascribed the fact that all the parts of the Body are joined
one with the other and with their exalted Head, for the
whole Spirit of Christ is in the Head, the *whole* Spirit is

[1] LG 8; CCC 771.
[2] DS 3013; CCC 812.

in the Body, and the *whole* Spirit is in each of the members."[3] The Holy Spirit is "the principle of every vital and truly saving action in each part of the Body".[4] That is why Charles Cardinal Journet, that great theologian of the Church, therefore, called the Holy Spirit "l'âme incréé de l'Église", the uncreated (that is, divine) soul of the Church, while he describes *love* as "l'âme créé de l'Église", the created soul of the Church.[5]

Among *all* the life-giving and truly saving actions that the Holy Spirit effects in the Church and her members (cf. CCC 798), *the theological virtues* are supreme.

> [T]he theological virtues relate directly to God. They dispose Christians to live in a relationship with the Holy Trinity. They have the One and Triune God for their origin, motive, and object. . . .
>
> The theological virtues are the foundation of Christian moral activity; they animate it and give it its special character. They inform and give life to all the moral virtues. They are infused by God into the souls of the faithful to make them capable of acting as his children and of meriting eternal life. They are the pledge of the presence and action of the Holy Spirit in the faculties of the human being (CCC 1812–13).

The *decisive* "manifestation" of the Church through the power of the Holy Spirit is to be found, therefore, in what theologians call the "theological life", in *faith, hope, and*

---

[3] Pope Pius XII, encyclical *Mystici corporis* (June 29, 1943) (DS 3808); CCC 797.

[4] Ibid.; CCC 798.

[5] See *Théologie de l'Église* (Bruges: Desclée de Brouwer, 1958), passim.

charity, those divine virtues that make us "partakers of the divine nature" (2 Pet 1:4), which *bring us into living "communion with Jesus Christ"* (CCC 426). Let us, therefore, devote our three remaining meditations today to the theological virtues. Needless to say, we can pick out only a few suggestions for personal meditation from this vast field of faith, hope, and charity. Let us begin with *faith.*

"*By faith*, man completely submits his intellect and his will to God. With his whole being man gives his assent to God the revealer. Sacred Scripture calls this human response to God, the author of revelation, 'the obedience of faith'" (CCC 143). That is how the Catechism "defines" faith. Someone might object to this definition, which is taken almost verbatim from *Dei verbum* 5, and say that it is too intellectual, too voluntaristic, that it does not give enough emphasis to *trust*, and so on. As a matter of fact, perhaps the definition does not make it sufficiently clear that the "assent" of the intellect and will is not something that happens as a merely human effort of the intellect and will. The *assent* of faith involves much more: actually *being moved* by God, having *real contact* with him, a true *participation* in God. This is the incomparable splendor of the theological virtues: they truly "attain" God in them, and through them we have a "*living union*" with the living triune God. It is precisely *because* the Church is "a people brought into unity from the unity of the Father, the Son, and the Holy Spirit"[6] that the theological virtues are the Church's *living environment.*

Saint John of the Cross can, therefore, say: "Faith gives

---

[6] St. Cyprian, *De Dominica oratione* 23; CCC 810.

us God himself and enables us to know him."[7] And again he says: "The more the soul has faith, the more it is united with God."[8] This also explains why Saint Thomas can say that faith is the *"inchoatio visionis"*, the beginning, albeit obscure, of the Beatific Vision of God.[9] Just as the Beatific Vision will unite us perfectly with God, so already faith unites us with him. There is no essential difference between faith and vision. Both *unite* us with God, faith in the darkness of our earthly journey, vision in the radiance of a sunlight without setting.

The great gift to the Church from the spiritual masters of Carmel is not only the many saints (so many, in fact, that a Dominican feels jealous!) but also the practice of *oración*, inner prayer, which these very saints lived and taught. What is *oración*? Simply a "living contact with God", and we attain this first of all through the act of faith. A great spiritual master of Carmel in our own century, the founder of the secular institute of Notre Dame de Vie, Father Marie-Eugène of the Child Jesus (let us hope he will soon be beatified), used a vivid image to speak of prayer: As surely as my hand will become wet if I plunge it into water, so my soul touches God when I make the act of faith. Whatever my physical or psychological state may be, "I know", says Saint Teresa of Avila, "that through the mere act of faith I can connect myself with God."[10]

Now it is one of the features of the theological virtues

---

[7] *The Spiritual Canticle*, st. 11.
[8] *The Ascent of Mount Carmel*, bk. 2, chap. 9, no. 1.
[9] Cf. STh 2a2ae 4, 1; cf. CCC 163.
[10] *The Way of Perfection*, chap. 28.

that they elude human experience. Do I have faith? Do I have hope and love? That cannot be determined by feelings, by psychological *experience*. The divine life in us is hidden, but that hiddenness does not make it any less real. Father Marie-Eugène of the Child Jesus says: "Whatever may be the psychological perception or absence of it, when a soul says 'I believe . . . on the authority of God', it has made a supernatural act; the virtue of faith has entered into action."[11]

The *Catechism* for its part says: "What *moves* us to believe is not the fact that revealed truths appear as true and intelligible in the light of our natural reason: we believe 'because of the authority of God himself who reveals them, who can neither deceive nor be deceived.' "[12] Believing because God is God and therefore infinitely *worthy of belief*: that is the *ground* of our faith. Yet it is God's own gift that makes it all possible: " 'Before this faith can be exercised, man must have the grace of God to move and assist him; he must have the interior helps of the Holy Spirit, who moves the heart and converts it to God, who opens the eyes of the mind and "makes it easy for all to accept and believe the truth." ' "[13]

Believing God is, therefore, an expression of reverence for God, indeed, of adoration of God, a confession that he truly is God: "I know *whom* I have believed" (2 Tim 1:12). But that is also why it is so important that our

---

[11] *I Want To See God: A Practical Synthesis of Carmelite Spirituality*, trans. Sister M. Verda Clare, C.S.C. (Notre Dame: Fides, 1953), 529.

[12] CCC 156, quoting Vatican Council I, *Dei Filius*, no. 3; DS 3008.

[13] CCC 153, quoting Vatican Council II, Dogmatic Constitution on Divine Revelation, *Dei Verbum* (November 18, 1965) no. 5.

proclamation should be an invitation to theological faith and should speak of it: this is substantial nourishment for the faithful.

As an entailment of our giving our credence to *God*, the Catechism teaches us the following lesson: "Faith is *certain*. It is more certain than all human knowledge because it is founded on the very word of God who cannot lie. To be sure, revealed truths can *seem obscure* to human reason and experience, but 'the certainty that the divine light gives is greater than that which the light of natural reason gives' [STh 2–2, 171, 5, obj. 3]. 'Ten thousand difficulties do not make one doubt' [John Henry Newman]" (CCC 157). That is why Saint John of the Cross defined faith as "a certain and obscure *habit* of the soul".[14] The Catechism goes on to say: "Even though enlightened by him in whom it believes, faith is often lived *in darkness* and can be put to the test. The world we live in often seems very far from the one promised us by faith. Our experiences of evil and suffering, injustice, and death, seem to contradict the Good News; they can shake our faith and become a temptation against it" (CCC 164).

In such trials let us turn to the witnesses of faith: to Abraham who believed "hoping against hope" (cf. Rom 4:18); and above all to *Mary*, who, in the words of the Council, walked by "the pilgrimage of faith".[15] In his meditation on the long years of the hidden life in the home in Nazareth, the Holy Father says that our Lady

---

[14] *The Ascent of Mount Carmel*, bk. 2, chap. 3, no. 1.
[15] LG 58; CCC 165.

is "in contact with the truth of her Son *only in faith and through faith*". He speaks of a "a sort of 'night of faith'" in Mary, "a kind of 'veil', through which one has to draw near to the Invisible One and to live in intimacy with the mystery".[16] Saint Thérèse of the Child Jesus had already spoken *explicitly*, in her last and longest poem, of Mary's having known the "night of faith".[17] What she speaks of there she had come to understand during the long months of her own "dark night": firm and peaceful faith can coexist with the deepest darkness of soul. In the *Novissima verba*, these words of Thérèse are reported: "I have read a beautiful passage in the meditations of *The Imitation of Christ* [of Thomas à Kempis]. In the Garden of Gethsemane, our Lord enjoyed all the delights of the Trinity, and yet his agony was no less terrible. This is a mystery, but I assure you that I understand something of it, because I experience it myself." If theological faith is this living contact with God, in which there is a real living communion with God, we can understand why faith is *necessary* to attain eternal life: "Without faith it is impossible to please [God]" (Heb 11:6). "[W]ithout faith no one has ever attained justification, nor will anyone obtain eternal life 'but he who endures to the end' [Mt 10:22; 24:13]."[18]

Imploring God for *the grace of perseverance* in faith demands that we recognize our weakness, still more that we have the desire to stay true to the love of God, the desire

---

[16] John Paul II, encyclical *Redemptoris Mater* (March 25, 1987), no. 17.

[17] "Pourquoi je t'aime, ô Marie", *Poésies*, no. 54, st. 15.

[18] Vatican I, DS 3012; CCC 161.

not to betray him: "Wage the good warfare, holding faith and a good conscience. By rejecting conscience, certain persons have made shipwreck of their faith [1 Tim 1:18–19]" (CCC 162).

I remember a meeting with Ignatius Cardinal Gon Pinmei, the Bishop of Shanghai, during his first visit to Rome and Lourdes. He had spent thirty-two years in prison because of his loyalty to the Pope. At the end of the meeting the then eighty-seven-year-old said that he had only one request of those present: "Pray for me, pray that I remain true to my faith to the end!" "O Lord, look not on *our sins*, but on the *faith of thy Church!*" In the face of the dangers to which our own faith is exposed both inwardly and outwardly, let us look upon *"the faith of God's Church"*. "No one can believe alone, just as no one can live alone. You have not given yourself faith as you have not given yourself life. . . . I cannot believe without being carried by the faith of others, and by my faith I help support others in the faith" (CCC 166). My faith, our faith, is not, of course, my faith, our faith, but *the* faith, the faith of *the Church. She* says "Credo", and I can only say that word with her: "It is the Church that believes first, and so bears . . . my faith" (CCC 168). "I believe": thus speaks the Church, our Mother, who by her faith responds to God and teaches us to say: "I believe", "we believe" (CCC 167). *Her* faith will not waver. *She* is "the pillar and bulwark of the truth" (1 Tim 3:15).

PRAISED BE JESUS CHRIST!

Third Meditation
Prayer—The Spokesman of Hope

Just before her conversion, Blessed Edith Stein went into the cathedral in Frankfurt and saw a simple woman come in from the market, kneel down, and pray. By Edith Stein's own testimony, the sight of this woman made a decisive impression upon her on her journey toward the faith: a simple woman, kneeling and praying in the cathedral. Something inexpressible, very simple, so ordinary, and yet so full of mystery: this intimate contact with the invisible God. Not a self-absorbed meditation, but quiet relaxation in the presence of a mysterious *Other*. What Edith Stein sensed in this humble praying woman would soon become a certainty for her: God exists, and in prayer we turn toward him.

Think of the impression the silent prayer of Jesus made on his disciples, prayer that often went on for hours, all night long, in fact! What was it about this secret place, this long turning in silence to him whom our Lord calls "Abba"? "He was praying in a certain place, and when he ceased, one of his disciples said to him, 'Lord, teach us to pray, as John taught his disciples'" (Lk 11:1). *Teach us to pray*. The disciple yearns to enter this place of silent intimacy, this vigilant prostration before the presence of the Invisible One. He feels such a great reverence for the mystery of the prayer of Jesus that he does not dare to interrupt, to "burst in" on our Lord with his question. He waits till Jesus himself comes out of his prayer. Only then does the disciple make bold to ask, to implore: "Teach us to pray!"

Does it not move us when we come into church and find someone silently praying there? Does this sight awaken in us the longing to pray? Do we hear at this moment the murmuring of the spring that summons us to the living water? As the martyr Ignatius of Antioch writes: "Living water murmurs within me, saying inwardly: 'Come to the Father!'"[1] *The longing for prayer is the lure within us of the Holy Spirit, who draws us to the Father. Yes, this longing is already prayer, is already the prayer of the Spirit of Christ within us, "with sighs too deep for words"* (Rom 8:26).

There is, of course, a question we have to consider carefully: Is the *ground* of prayer dried up today? Isn't the hidden "murmuring" of the wellspring of the Holy Spirit drowned out by the noise of our times? Can prayer prosper when, as Neil Postman writes in his disturbing book *Amusing Ourselves to Death*, the average American spends fifteen years of his life in front of the television? Isn't it a little hint from Divine Providence that "by chance" the canon in the Code with the number of the Beast in the Apocalypse (666) is the one that warns religious (and presumably not just them) of the misuse of the mass media and points out the possible dangers for one's religious vocation? There is no doubt that there is much in today's society that is detrimental to prayer.

[1] *Epistula ad Romanos* 7, 2.

And yet we are permitted to *hope* that no secularization can entirely drown out the call of God in the hearts of men. When I see the countless candles in Saint Stephen's Cathedral in Vienna burning day in, day out, by the altar of Our Lady of Pötsch, I think to myself that they can be regarded as a visible sign of the fact that prayer is not dead. For prayer is the expression of a longing, which has not been "produced" by *us* but has been placed in the hearts of men by God. It is an expression of the "fecisti nos *ad Te*" of Saint Augustine (Thou madest us *for thyself*). The candles in the cathedral by the miraculous image of the Mother of God are *witnesses of hope. He who prays, hopes.* For someone who cannot hope to be heard cannot ask. After all we only ask other human beings for something when we have the hope that our petition has a chance of being granted. "Prayer", says Saint Thomas, "is the spokesman of hope."[2] This is the theme of our second meditation on the theological virtues.

By our prayer we can gauge the state of our prayer. For what do we pray? For what do we hope? The reason why prayer and hope are so closely related is that both realize that what we pray and hope for does not lie within our own powers but can only be *given* to us. But what are we permitted to hope for? And what should we pray for? In his long *quaestio* on prayer (the longest in the whole *Summa*), Saint Thomas says:

> Since prayer is a kind of spokesman for our desires with God, we only ask for something in prayer rightly if we

[2] STh 2a2ae 17, 4, obj. 3.

desire it rightly. In the Lord's Prayer not only do we ask for all that we may rightly desire, we also ask for them in the order in which we are supposed to desire them. This prayer, then, not only teaches us to ask, it also shapes all our affections (*sit informativa totius nostri affectus*).[3]

A wonderful statement: The Our Father shapes our whole affective life into its right proportions; it places in us desires and yearnings and therefore the right priorities in our praying.

Is it really reasonable for our primary hope, and therefore our greatest longing, to be: "*Thy* Kingdom come, *thy* will be done"? We have a concern for our "daily bread" (think how many of our people are worrying about their jobs or have already lost them!). We want to get on well with one another ("Forgive us our trespasses . . ."). Above all, we beg for protection from evil and temptation, from anguish and despair ("Lead us not into temptation", "Deliver us from evil"). All of these petitions develop out of the problems of our life. They force their way to the front of our attention and harass our hearts. They are usually, therefore, our first and most pressing petitions.

The fact that we turn to *God* with these petitions shows that we expect, that we *hope* for, help from him in all these needs. As Cardinal Ratzinger has said, prayer is "hope in action", for "prayer is the language of hope."[4] "The de-

---

[3] STh 2a2ae 83, 9.

[4] *Auf Christus schauen: Einübung un Glaube, Hoffnung, Liebe* (Freiburg im Breisgau: Herder, 1989), 68f.

spairing man no longer prays, because he no longer hopes. The man who is sure of himself and his own strength does not pray, because he relies only on himself. The man who prays hopes for a good and for a strength that go beyond his own powers."[5] If we really pray for what we ask for in the four petitions of the second part of the Our Father, then we are already *hoping*, and that hope goes beyond the thing we ask for, it is directed toward the *Person* of whom we ask it: "Hallowed be *thy* name, *thy* Kingdom come, *thy* will be done. . . ." These petitions become the articulation of an ever greater trust, which dares to call God "Our Father".

Saint Thomas says that the Our Father is "informativa totius nostri affectus": it shapes all our desires and feelings. And indeed, time and again, we hear of people being healed in the very roots of their lives through the Our Father. I am thinking, for example, of Alexander Solzhenitsyn's friend Dimitri Panin,[6] or of Tatiana Gorischeva, who received the grace of conversion through reciting the Our Father. When our *affectus* is shaped by the Our Father, our desires and yearnings are sound and in conformity to the action of God, and then our prayer will be more and more efficacious, because it really will be in harmony with God's plan, really will be cooperating with God's Providence. Then our praying will be in harmony with the "sighs" of the Spirit, who "intercedes for the saints according to the will of God" (Rom 8:27). In

[5] Ibid., 69.

[6] See *The Notebooks of Sologdin* (New York: Harcourt Brace Jovanovich, 1976).

the *Compendium theologiae*, Saint Thomas says: "The Our Father is the prayer through which our hope in God is raised up to the highest degree."[7]

But what is *hope*? "Hope is the theological virtue by which we desire the kingdom of heaven and eternal life as our happiness, placing our trust in Christ's promises and relying not on our own strength, but on the help of the grace of the Holy Spirit" (CCC 1817). Josef Pieper says very simply: "Hope is the confidently patient expectation of eternal beatitude in a contemplative and comprehensive sharing of the triune life of God."[8] More simply still, Cajetan, commenting on Thomas, says: "Spes sperat Deum a Deo" (hope hopes for God from God).[9] Hope looks toward the eternal indestructible happiness of God himself. It does not hope for something, but for Someone, *for God himself*, the giver of all gifts. It does not *see*, nor does it *possess*, but it reaches out *to God himself*. Hope, so to speak, "drops its anchor" and is "moored" in God.

Just as faith is *certain*, because it believes *God*, so hope does not disappoint (cf. Rom 5:5), because, full of trust, it expects *from God* what he promises. It is from God *alone* that hope derives its triumphant certainty: "In *te*, Domine speravi, non confundar in aeternum" (In *thee*, O Lord, have I trusted, let me never be confounded). How marvellously Anton Bruckner sets this closing verse of

[7] *Compendium theologiae* 2, 3.

[8] *Faith, Hope, Love*, trans. Richard and Clara Winston and Sr. Mary Frances McCarthy, S.N.D. (San Francisco: Ignatius Press, 1997), 103.

[9] Commentary on 2a2ae 17, 5.

the Te Deum! If prayer is "hope in action", then the difficulties and dangers we encounter in prayer are also problems of hope. According to the great Christian spiritual masters, *desperatio* and *praesumptio*, *despair* (having too little hope) and *presumption* (having false hopes) are the wrong attitudes in opposition to hope.

I should like to speak here of one kind of wrong attitude that comes close to *despair*. It especially besets us ecclesiastics. It threatens our spiritual life. It robs hope of its zest: *acedia*, "accidie", "spiritual torpor", of which I spoke briefly on the evening of the first day.

What do we mean by *acedia*? It is closely related to anger and sadness.

> Generally speaking, accidie is, first of all, an *enervation*, a kind of *loss of voltage* in the natural powers of the soul making a man unable to defend himself against the "thoughts" that so violently attack him. All the . . . aspects of accidie . . . result from this general inertia: the feeling of emptiness and boredom, the inability to fix one's mind on something definite, disgust and distaste for everything and anything, gloomy brooding, weariness, and anguish of heart.[10]

The ancients called *acedia* the "midday demon", because it attacked the monk especially during the broodingly hot midday hours. It is a peculiar blend of *frustration* and *aggression*: disgust with what is *at hand*, vague dreaming about what is *not at hand*. It is a kind of *blind alley* in the life of the soul.[11]

---

[10] G. Bunge, *Akedia: Die geistliche Lehre des Evagrios Pontikos von Überdruss* (Cologne: Luthe, 1989), 38.

[11] Cf. ibid., 45.

It is hard not to be shocked when the old experienced monks describe the temptations of *acedia*—with seriousness, but also with self-irony. Accidie shows itself in a kind of spiritual sluggishness but, at the same time, often in hectic busyness. Flight from one's cell—that seems to have been the compulsion of the monks, but it is not hard to see how such *acedia* can show itself in the situations of our own lives as well—*in the form of anxiety about being on one's own, as fear of oneself, of silence*. *Verbositas* and *curiositas*, *garrulousness* and *curiosity* are the "daughters" of *acedia*: inner restlessness, an incessant quest for the new as a substitute for joy in God and his love, unsteadiness in life and in one's resolutions. And then *acedia* branches out into other inclinations: spiritual deadening (*torpor*) toward the things of faith and the presence of the Lord; faintheartedness (*pusillanimitas*), resentment (*rancor*) (which is so common among us in the Church these days), even deliberate wickedness (*malitia*).

Are such things not a constant temptation for us, an enticement by the demon of *acedia*? In today's terminology, we would call it "frustration" and "aggression". "A downcast spirit dries up the bones" (Prov 17:22). Are we not threatened by such spiritual drying up? Does not much of the complaining about the Church and anger with the Church come from such *acedia*? It threatens our life by letting the soul sink into morbid self-centeredness. It eats up the life of prayer and so robs our spiritual life of the very air it breathes.

The ancient masters of the spiritual life recognized *one* remedy above all others against the *hopelessness* that we call *acedia*. That remedy is long-suffering, patience, *hy-*

pomonē in its literal sense of abiding beneath the yoke. *Long-suffering is already an expression of hope.* It refuses to solve problems by any kind of attempt at break-out and escape, which does not set us free from the chains of self-absorption but often entangles us in them more deeply. No, we have to "wait upon God", look toward him patiently and faithfully in prayer. Such waiting amid the dark trials of *acedia* is like walking in thick fog. Everything seems blurred, with no way forward and no way out. But then suddenly the fog begins to break. The sun burns it away, and brilliant daylight shines forth. So it is with the temptation of *acedia*. Suddenly it disappears, and one is left with deep peace and unutterable joy. Hope has triumphed.

In the life of Saint Antony there is an episode that gives us an impressive description of how the saint waited patiently till the "fog cleared". After a long period of temptation, Antony asks reproachfully: "Lord, where were you all that time? Why did you not immediately appear to relieve my pains?" Then Antony hears the answer: "I was there, Antony! But I waited to see your struggle."[12]

Hope, said Father Marie-Eugène, is "the virtue of progress in the spiritual life; it is the motor that keeps it moving, the wings that lift it up".[13] *Acedia* always has to do with *disappointed self-love* and so is a vice of the "rich", who get to feel all the "sorrows of the world". By contrast, *hope* has something to do with "*poverty of*

---

[12] *Vita Antonii*, cap. 10.
[13] Fr. Marie-Eugène de l'Enfant Jésus, *I Am a Daughter of the Church*, trans. Sr. M. Verda Clare, C.S.C. (Notre Dame: Fides, 1955), 380.

spirit". The great doctor of hope, on the threshold of this century so deep in despair, is Saint Thérèse of the Child Jesus. Her "way of childhood", her "Little Way", displays vividly and practically the way to live out the virtue of hope. To the question, "What way do you want to teach souls?", Thérèse answers without hesitation: "The way of spiritual childhood, the way of trust and total abandonment."[14] One of the most important "nutshell definitions" of the Little Way runs as follows: "We can *never* have too great a trust in God's love, who is so powerful and merciful. *We receive* from Him as much as one hopes of Him."

Hope, then, means thinking *great* things of God, expecting great things of God. For Thérèse, its presupposition is love of one's own poverty: "It is *Jesus* who *does everything* in me, and I do nothing."[15] "Even if I had accomplished all the works of Saint Paul, I should still think myself to be a 'useless servant' (Lk 17:10), but that is precisely what gives me joy, *for having nothing*, I shall receive everything from the good God."[16] For Thérèse, this definitely does not mean being purely passive. For her, being poor means receiving all ability and activity, even determined effort, as gift. This poverty makes her seek a constant contact with God: "In fact, *my hope has never been disappointed. The good God has deigned to fill my little hand, as often as necessary, to nourish the souls of my sisters.*"[17] Seldom

[14] *Derniers entretiens*, July 17, 1897.
[15] Letter to Céline, July 6, 1893.
[16] *Derniers entretiens*, June 23, 1897.
[17] *Autobiographical Writings*, Manuscript C, 22v.

has the first Beatitude been so clearly, so decisively lived: "Blessed are the poor in spirit, for theirs is the kingdom of heaven" (Mt 5:3), that is to say, God himself.

To conclude, one last, very profound summary of the *Little Way*: "God likes to see me loving my littleness and my poverty, *my blind hope in His mercy* [*l'espérance aveugle en sa miséricorde*]. . . . That is my only treasure. *Why should it not be yours too?*" [18]

PRAISED BE JESUS CHRIST!

---

[18] Letter to Sr. Marie of the Sacred Heart, September 17, 1896.

Fourth Meditation
The Love That Is Friendship

The Church of Jesus Christ, says the Council, is the "community of faith, hope, and love". "So faith, hope, love abide, these three; but the greatest of these is love" (1 Cor 13:13). *Love* is the innermost life of the Church, for God is love, and God is the life of the Church.

There is much that we could consider in this connection. For this final meditation of the fourth day of these exercises, I should like to take Saint Thomas Aquinas as "choirmaster", just as Saint Thérèse was our conductor on the theme of hope. And here again I should like to place at the center of our thoughts a text from the *Summa theologiae* of Saint Thomas. This text, so it seems to me, is the very *heart* of the whole of the *Summa*, the keystone that holds the entire building together. Even though the Church is not directly discussed, this passage is nonetheless concerned with the Church's *innermost principle of life*, from which all her *manifestations of life* derive their power. But before we turn to *quaestio* 23 of the *Secunda Secundae* of the *Summa*, let me give you two mottos for our meditation:

1. On the night before his Passion, our Lord said to his disciples: "No longer do I call you servants, for the servant does not know what his master is doing; *but I*

have called you friends, for *all* that I have heard from my Father *I have made known* to you" (Jn 15:15).

2. Saint Teresa of Avila defined *oración*, interior prayer, as follows: "Contemplative prayer, in my opinion, is nothing else than a close *sharing between friends*; it means taking time frequently to be alone with him who we know loves us."[1] "Utrum caritas sit amicitia?" (Is charity friendship?) So begins the first and most important question of Saint Thomas' treatise on the theological virtue of charity. The sober language of the *Doctor communis* should not deceive us. Here speaks a *burning heart*, which is indeed entirely "objective", gazing self-forgetfully at the *one and only* "object" of his contemplation, at God alone, and at other things in relation to God as their beginning and end.[2]

"Not every love is friendship." The love that is friendship has two distinguishing characteristics: *benevolentia*, that is to say, willing the good of the other person; and *mutua amatio*, mutuality of love. Not every love has these qualities. Friendship presupposes a certain *equality*. There is no friendship without mutual exchange: "A friend is a friend to his friend [*amicus amico amicus*]", says Thomas with Aristotle, "Talis mutua benevolentia fundatur super aliquam communicationem" (Such mutual good will is based on some kind of communication).[3]

But can there be a *mutual* loving between God and man? "Infiniti ad finitum nulla est proportio." How can

[1] *Vida* 8, 5; CCC 2709.
[2] Cf. STh Ia I, 7.
[3] STh 2a2ae 23, I.

there be friendship between the infinitely different? Saint Thomas' answer is, so it seems to me, the very center of the *Summa*: "There is a certain communication, communion, of man with God, because God communicates to us his beatitude. Upon this communion *a friendship* has to be built."[4] There is a *real* communication (*communicatio*) of God with man: a real participation in his life, his beatitude (*beatitudo*). God gives himself so that upon this gift *a friendship* might be built. *Fundari amicitiam*—is this not God's entire plan, from the beginning of creation to the hour when Jesus says to his disciples: "I have called you friends, for all that I have heard from my Father I have *made known* to you" (Jn 15:15).

Friendship is the sharing and communicating of what is most precious to us. Jesus no longer calls the disciples "servants", "for the servant does not know what his master is doing". He calls them "friends", because he has entrusted to them the innermost secret of his life: his love for the Father in the Holy Spirit. They become his friends, because they participate in this mystery, not only in knowledge, but with their lives. All growth in Christian life, the whole work of the Church, has its meaning and goal in this *fundari amicitiam*.

But what is this *communicatio*? In other words, what is this share in God's own happiness that friendship with God makes possible for us? It is *grace*, of which Thomas says: "Gratia nihil aliud est quam quaedam inchoatio gloriae in nobis" (Grace is nothing other than a kind of be-

---

[4] "Cum ergo sit aliqua communicatio hominis ad Deum secundum quod nobis suam beatitudinem communicat, super hanc communicationem oportet aliquam amicitiam fundari", ibid.

ginning of glory in us).[5] It is the way we can be, *even now*, in a *communion of life* with God that gives us a true happiness. Saint Paul never tires of praising God's "glorious grace", its overflowing "riches" (Eph 1:6–7). Saint Dominic, the Father of my Order, is acclaimed as the *praedicator gratiae*, "the Preacher of Grace", just as Saint Augustine is regarded as the *doctor gratiae*, "the Doctor of Grace". "Tout est grâce", all is grace, so Saint Thérèse sums up the whole Christian life. But what is grace? What is this communication of God himself to man, through which we can become *friends of God*? Saint Thomas approaches this question with a surprising discussion. *Peter Lombard*, the Master of the Sentences, had said that charity is *the Holy Spirit himself*, dwelling in the soul. When we love God, the Holy Spirit himself directly moves our love.[6] That sounds very "pious", but when you look at it more closely, says Thomas, you realize it does damage to love. If Lombard were right, then charity in us would not be *our* love for God. We would be things passively moved, not persons loving God *ourselves*. No *friendship* could result if we were unable to love God *ourselves* and in freedom. For there to be a real *friendship with God*, "our will must be so moved to love by the Holy Spirit that our will, too, performs this act."

How is our human will, our human power, supposed to produce acts that really "attain" and touch God? For all our human acts are sustained and made possible by faculties that incline us toward their proper activities. To

[5] STh 24, 3, ad 2.
[6] STh 23, 2.

be able to *love* God (and the same applies to faith and hope), we need a God-given "talent" and ability, going beyond our natural capacities, which will *incline* us to the act of charity ("inclinans ad caritatis actum"), enabling us to love promptly and with joy. Grace makes us friends of God. It creates the foundation on which a friendship with God can be built (*fundari amicitiam*). God gives us a share in his own *beatitudo*, his *life*, and so we truly become "like him" and can become his friends.

Let me add *three comments*:

1. According to Saint Thomas, every virtue makes us inclined toward its proper activity. That is why the characteristic of virtue is a certain joy and ease. Of no virtue is this more true than charity: "Nulla virtus habet tantam inclinationem ad suum actum sicut caritas, nec aliqua ita delectabiliter operatur" (No virtue has so great an inclination to its act as charity, nor does any operate so delightfully).[7] Love loves to love, and nothing gives it greater joy. No activity is more fitting to man than loving. Nothing is more joyful, more fulfilling, than the love that is friendship with God.

2. Saint Thomas teaches us that charity is the "forma omnium virtutum" (form of all the virtues). Charity gives all the virtues their *soul*, their vitality. Here Saint Thomas says only what the Apostle says: Without charity, even the most heroic virtues are *nothing*, in fact *not* really virtues ". . . if I have not love" (1 Cor 13:1ff.). That is why Saint

[7] Ibid.

Thomas can also say that charity is the life principle of the soul, just as the soul is the life principle of the body.[8] Love is, therefore, also the God-given *life principle* of the Church. It is her standard, by which everything within her, including us her members, are measured. John of the Cross says: "At the evening of life, we shall be judged on our love."[9] May we then be able to say what Saint Thérèse said in suffering her final agony, just a few moments before she died: "Je ne me repens pas de m'être livrée à l'Amour" (I do not regret having given myself up to Love).[10]

3. *Amor amicitiae.* The friendship that God makes possible by his grace causes a certain "connaturality" with him, a kind of "kinship", a familiarity. It is not the kind of familiarity that can be sensed or perceived, but it does live and act by means of a *feeling for God.* The deeper our friendship with God becomes, the more surely it enables us to judge and act according to the mind of God. It gives us that unerring sense of truth and goodness that constitutes the *sensus fidelium*, the People of God's "supernatural sense of faith" (LG 12). Saint Thomas speaks of the "indicium per connaturalitatem", (evidence by connaturality). It is the right judgment, the good sense, of the "little ones" of the Gospel, for whom Jesus praises the Father (cf. Mt 11:25, 27). Thomas speaks of the "instinctus Spiritus Sancti", which accurately detects what is

[8] STh 23, 2, ad 2.
[9] *Dichos*, no. 64; CCC 1022.
[10] *Derniers entretiens*, September 30, 1897.

correct in matters of faith, hope, and charity. The friends of God see, understand, sense everything "with the eyes of a friend". They know with the heart of God.

Just one final thought. If the love of God makes us friends with him, it also makes us friends *with one another.* When Jesus calls the Twelve his "friends", that is bound to have implications for their relationships with one another. How could the *spirit of friendship* not hold sway among them, these men to whom Christ had entrusted what was most precious to him? In our own times, when affectivity has been wounded in so many ways, when so many of the faithful, so many priests, are suffering from such wounds, the theme of friendship in Christ acquires a new urgency. Communion with Christ, *friendship with him*, not only reconciles men with God, frees them from their sins, and heals the consequences of their sins, it also heals—though only with much patience—their relationships with each other. *Friendship* here plays an essential role. It is endangered by all kinds of deviations —superficiality, the eroticizing and sexualizing of everything, emotional impoverishment. All the more clearly do the beauty and healing power of Christian friendship stand out.

It has its place between married people, for married love, if it is to grow and to last, needs the love that is friendship. But also in the lives of those who are unmarried, whether voluntarily or unintentionally, friendship is the way of the healing and unfolding of the heart. Jacques Maritain once wrote this beautiful sentence to Julien Green: "God asks certain persons to become eunuchs for the Kingdom, but he doesn't ask them to amputate their hearts."[11] But for the heart to be capable of friendship in Christ, it needs purification. It must mature into the *amor benevolentiae*, become free from the *amor concupiscentiae*, which wants to possess, to have, the other person for itself. An unerring sign of such friendship in Christ is its capacity to pass on friendship, to cast out the net of friendship to others. *Madeleine Delbrêl* speaks of the Church as *Peter's fishing net*: knit together of many friendships in Christ, by him it can be cast out to make a wonderful catch of fish.

Sin has given the world the taste of death. The Church brings back to the world a taste for life. Saint Catherine of Siena says: "We cannot live without love, for we are of the stuff of love."[12] Today there are Christian families and married couples who are reawakening in the people of our time the desire to transmit life. But in our world of unrelenting competition and rivalry, the Church is also called to reawaken the taste of the *love that is friendship*. "Married love is a source transmitting life. The love that is friendship is an 'elixir of life' (cf. Sir 6:16), that is to say, it makes you want to go on living."[13] "Through love in marriage and in friendship, our Christian life, our Church communities, sow the world with the taste of

[11] "Dieu demande à certaines personnes de devenir eunuques pour le royaume, mais il ne leur demande pas de s'amputer le coeur" (*Julien Green et Jacques Maritain: Une grande amitié: Correspondance, 1926–1972* [Paris: Gallimard, 1982], 79).

[12] *The Dialogue*, nos. 51 and 10.

[13] "Si l'amour conjugal est une source qui transmet la vie, l'amour d'amitié est un élixir de vie, c'est-à-dire ce qui donne envie de continuer à vivre" (J. M. Garrigues, *Ce Dieu qui passe par les hommes*, vol. 1 [Paris, 1992], 55).

life, with the taste of the *hope* that life is not headed for destruction but toward the final splendor of the wedding feast of heaven."[14]

PRAISED BE JESUS CHRIST!

[14] Ibid., 56.

THE CHURCH WILL BE PERFECTED IN GLORY AT THE END OF TIME

First Meditation
The Pilgrim Church

"The Church . . . will receive its perfection only in the glory of heaven [LG 48]," at the time of Christ's glorious return. Until that day, "the Church progresses on her pilgrimage amidst this world's persecutions and God's consolations".[1] Here below she knows that she is in exile far from the Lord, and longs for the full coming of the Kingdom, when she will "be united in glory with her king" [LG 5]. The Church, and through her the world, will not be perfected in glory without great trials. Only then will "all the just from the time of Adam, 'from Abel, the just one, to the last of the elect,' . . . be gathered together in the universal Church in the Father's presence" [LG 2] (CCC 769).

With these words the Catechism touches on all the themes that we are to consider today, the last day of our spiritual exercises:

1. The Church has not yet been perfected. She is *on pilgrimage* on earth, "far from the Lord".

[1] St. Augustine, *De civitate Dei* 18, 51.

2. But on her pilgrim way the Church does not lack "God's consolations": she lives in the *communio sanctorum*.

3. "Not . . . without great trials" will the Church attain her perfection. We shall discuss this when we look at the coming Great Jubilee.

4. The Church yearns to be united with her Lord and King, her Bridegroom. This will be the theme of our last meditation this evening.

The seventh chapter of *Lumen Gentium* is one of the least considered parts of the Dogmatic Constitution on the Church, and yet in a sense it is the key to the second chapter on the People of God. The image of the journeying People of God would be a "blind" image if we forgot the *destination* of that journey. The final destination has still not been reached. The Church is still on the road. But she knows what her destination is. She stretches out toward it. *She yearns for Christ.*

When I was young, we often sang a hymn in church with a special, almost palpable atmosphere of devotion—or at least that was my impression. This is how the first verse went: "We are but guests upon the earth, unresting e'er we roam; 'mid tribulations without dearth, we seek our Father's home." The hymn has largely gone out of use. The criticism could be heard that it was all about *fuga mundi*, flight from the world, that now we have to devote ourselves to *this* world. For a long time we heard the reproach—for example, from the Marxist side—that we Christians were consoling people with the afterlife, with happiness after death, instead of struggling against unhappiness and getting rid of suffering before death. It goes to show, they said, that religion is "the opium of the people".

Something very strange has taken place in the last few years: Christians have lost touch with heaven! Of the desire for heaven, our "heavenly home", we hear hardly a word. It is as if Christians have lost the *orientation* that for centuries defined the direction of their journey. We have forgotten that we are pilgrims and that the goal of our pilgrimage is heaven. Connected with this is another loss: we largely lack the awareness that we are on a *dangerous* pilgrim path and that it is possible for us to miss our goal, to fail to reach the goal of our life. To put it bluntly: we do not long for heaven; we take it for granted that we shall get there. This diagnosis may be exaggerated, overstated. The trouble is, I am afraid it is essentially true.

Against this loss and neglect, the Church's Easter message proclaims: "If . . . you have been raised with Christ, seek the things that are above, where Christ is, seated at the right hand of God" (Col 3:1). "My desire is to depart and be with Christ" (Phil 1:23). This profound and pressing yearning does not strive for just any kind of "life after death" but is the desire "to be with Christ", to live with him, to be "at home with the Lord": "So we are always of good courage; we know that while we are at home in the body, we are *away from* the Lord, for we walk by faith, not by sight. We are of good courage, and we would rather be away from the body and *at home with the Lord*" (2 Cor 5:6–8).

"At home"! For so many people, who have lost their

homes or their homeland, the word "home" is a word
of longing. The English word "home" (home town or
homeland), like the German *Heimat*, has a strongly emotional, almost devotional resonance, which we do not find
in the Latin *patria* or the French *patrie*. "Home" is not just
a particular landscape, not just its language, its familiar
landmarks, but above all the people who live there. When
the people we were familiar with (friends, neighbors, ac-
quaintances) no longer live there, then "home" has died,
even if the landscape has remained. How often have the
great artists and writers of our century expressed their
pain at *the loss of their homelands*. So many people have
eaten the bitter bread of exile.

The Church is the *promise of home*. The man who has
found the Church has found his way home. Paul speaks of
this new home: "*Our* home [*politeuma*] is in heaven" (Phil
3:20). Our home is in heaven, because it is in heaven that
we find *our true family*. That is why Paul tells the faithful
in Ephesus: "You are no longer strangers and sojourners,
but you are *fellow citizens* with the saints and *members of
the household* of God" (Eph 2:19). And we have found
a Mother: "[T]he Jerusalem above . . . is our mother"
(Gal 4:26). Home also means having a *house to live in*: "In
my Father's house are many rooms . . . I go to prepare
a place for you. And when I go and prepare a place for
you, I will come again and will take you to myself, that
where I am you may be also" (Jn 14:2–3).

The Church is first of all, then, a "heavenly reality".
She has her origin in the life of God himself, in the unity
of the Blessed Trinity, and so, in the words of Hans Urs
von Balthasar, she is "first and foremost a reality estab-

lished in time from heaven".[2] The foundations of the Church are "above", which is why Saint Augustine says: "Since our foundation [Christ] is in heaven, let us be built up toward heaven . . . for we are built spiritually, and our foundation lies above. Let us hasten, therefore, whither we are built."[3]

This look of longing toward the heavenly homeland is not an escape from our earthly responsibilities. On the contrary, hope for heaven, for full communion with Christ "and all the angels and saints", is the very *motor*, the driving force, of Christian engagement in this world. Christian hope for the coming of God's Kingdom asks for both things from God: that his Kingdom may come in glory (or, as the *Didachē* prays, "that grace may come and the world pass away");[4] and that his Kingdom may begin already *here* on earth.

The *consequences* of this view of the Church as our *heavenly homeland* will be addressed in what I am about to say. Further aspects will be discussed in today's three remaining meditations.

1. There is an astonishing statement in *Lumen Gentium*: "[U]ntil there be realized new heavens and a new earth in which justice dwells [cf. 2 Pet 3:13], the pilgrim Church, in her sacraments and institutions, *which belong to this present age*, carries the mark of this world which will pass, and she herself takes her place among the creatures which groan and travail yet and await the revelation of the sons of

---

[2] *Theodramatik*, vol. 4 (Einsiedeln: Johannes Verlag, 1983), 114.

[3] *Enarrationes in Psalmos*, 121, 4.

[4] *Didachē* 10, 6.

God [cf. Rom 8:19–22].''[5] The Church's ''pilgrim garb'' belongs to *this world*, to the form of *this* world that is passing away. Just as there will be no longer any sacrament of matrimony in Heaven (cf. Mt 22:30), so the whole sacramental and institutional order of the Church belongs to the time of the Church's pilgrimage. What will *abide* is what the sacraments and institutions signify and effect in the divine life. What will *pass away* is the form of the signs.

If the Church's orientation toward her heavenly home is ignored or neglected, there is a *double danger*, which is only too clearly evident today.

a. *On the one hand*, the Church's ''established'' aspects are overvalued: her institutions, her organization are given too much weight. An often alarmingly pragmatic and horizontal understanding of the Church becomes widespread. The Church is seen too much as a human work, too little as the place of grace. This is the source of much of the groaning and complaining, the outrage and anger and disappointment with the Church. Were we to see our way as the Church's *pilgrim way*, as a sighing and groaning with the whole of creation, then much would be more easily and gladly borne. The knowledge that on earth we are pilgrims also protects us from the utopias of a Church already ideal and perfected here on earth.[6]

b. *On the other hand*, the danger also exists today that, because of overemphasis on the institutional aspect, we do not sufficiently perceive that the *sacramental pilgrim-*

---

[5] LG 48; CCC 671.
[6] I shall speak of this in the third of today's meditations.

form of the Church *already contains within it all the riches of the heavenly homeland,* albeit "in earthen vessels" (cf. 2 Cor 4:7). As Hans Urs von Balthasar says: "Without doubt the Church on earth is a largely visible earthly reality, just as we men who adhere to her are, just as Jesus Christ was when he walked on earth. But as it was with Jesus Christ, so it is with the Church: *the most important thing about her* remains invisible, just as the divinity of the Christ who walked on earth was invisible and only accessible to faith."[7]

The Catechism makes the same point: "The Church is in history, but at the same time she transcends it. It is only 'with the eyes of faith' that one can see her in her visible reality and at the same time in her spiritual reality as bearer of divine life" (CCC 770).

The sacraments are the clearest example of this need to see the Church "with the eyes of faith". Saint Augustine speaks of the "humilitas sacramentorum" (the humility of the Sacraments), when he is describing the spiritual struggle of the learned Marius Victorinus. Victorinus was afraid that, if he submitted to baptism, he would be ridiculed by the top people of his time, but then he began to be even more afraid that Christ might one day disown him before the angels if he was now afraid to confess Christ before men. And so Marius Victorinus overcame the shame he felt before the "sacraments of the humility of thy God [*humilitatis Verbi tui*]".[8] And how beautifully Augustine spoke of his friend Alypius, who, with Au-

---

[7] Hans Urs von Balthasar, *Homo creatus est*. Skizzen zur Theologie, 5 (Einsiedeln: Johannes Verlag, 1986), 149.

[8] *Confessiones* 8, 2, 4.

gustine himself and Adeodatus, was ready to be baptized, because "he was already endowed with the humility that befits thy sacraments [*induto humilitate sacramentis tuis congrua*]."[9]

The *superbia* that will not accept the humble form of Christ's grace in the sacraments can assume many forms apart from the intellectual pride, linked with fear of men, of Marius Victorinus. The common temptation today is to look for *experience* rather than the simple self-surrender of faith. "The man who wants experience at any price is thinking more of himself than of God. The man who throws himself in faith and love into the words and events of the Church's life—for example, into what the Eucharistic Prayer really says—such a man is orientated toward God and has been taken hold of by God without having specially to strive for it."[10]

There is an even more subtle temptation to evade the "humilitas sacramentorum": expecting the *visible* form of the Church in her sacraments and institutions to be "convincing to men", to be impressive in their strength and competence, in their beauty and historical splendor. The Church should be *attractive*, *winning*, should find approval. In a society dominated by the "media", *this* temptation can grow into an obsession: public recognition, media recognition, becomes the yardstick. "But if it is true that the primordial significance of the Church's institutions is that they make possible the hidden divine life, then we really should not expect the institutions to have a partic-

---

[9] Ibid., 9, 6, 14.
[10] Balthasar, *Homo creatus est*, 154.

ularly attractive and apologetical effect. Men do not turn toward the Church because of her institutions, for they are only signs and foreshadowings of something primarily invisible, the saving power of God, which is at work in a hidden way within them."[11] And here we see a surprising thing: the man who is not spellbound by the success of the Church's institutions, but looks for the invisible saving power hidden within them, will time and again see something of "omnis gloria eius ab intus", all of the Church's glory coming from within, shining forth in her external accouterments.

Anyone who looks for the Church's success in her institutions is easily disappointed, indeed, embittered. He is hoping for fruit from peel, is confusing the tough peel with the fruit it protects and contains. On the other hand, if we are to endure and tolerate the everyday troubles of our Church institutions, it will help us if we recognize the institutions as the necessary peel of the fruit within. This humble service of the pilgrim-form of the Church—the kind of service faithfully performed precisely *here*, in the Vatican, year in, year out, unnoticed and unglamorous —can begin to shine from within when it is animated by faith, hope, and charity. The "Little Way" of Saint Thérèse can light up the everyday life of our Church institutions. *That* is when Church reform takes place, the renewal that alone rejuvenates the Church on her pilgrim way, of which Saint Irenaeus says: "We guard with care *the faith* that we have received from the Church, for, without ceasing, under the action of God's Spirit, this deposit

[11] Ibid., 151f.

of great price, as if in an excellent vessel, *is constantly being renewed and causes the very vessel that contains it to be renewed.*" [12]

PRAISED BE JESUS CHRIST!

---

[12] *Adversus haereses* 3, 24, 1; CCC 175.

Second Meditation
The Communion of Saints

"What is the Church", says Nicetas of Remesiana, "if not the assembly of the saints?" He explains this statement in a way that sounds like a summary of our whole retreat so far:

> Since the beginning of the world, the Patriarchs . . . , the Prophets, the Martyrs, and all the just . . . form *one single Church*, since, being sanctified by one and the same faith and with one and the same life, and being signed with the sign of one and the same Spirit, they form one single Body, of which Body, as it is written, Christ is the Head. . . . *Even the angels*, even the Virtues and Powers above, are *members of this one Church*. . . . Believe, therefore, that in this one Church you have attained the Communion of Saints. Know, too, that this Catholic Church is one, established all over the world. You must hold fast and resolutely to communion with her.[1]

Our second meditation on this last day is devoted to the *communio sanctorum*. It is *one* of the names of the Church. It describes that "living union" with Christ (cf. CCC 426) that we have been considering during these days as the *mystery* of the Church's *life*. "The term 'communion of saints' therefore has two closely linked meanings:

[1] *Explanatio symboli* 10; PL 52, 871.

185

communion 'in holy things (*sancta*)' and 'among holy persons (*sancti*)'" (CCC 948). Both meanings are heard in the cry of the celebrant in the liturgies of the Eastern Churches when he elevates the Eucharistic Gifts before Holy Communion: "*Ta hagia tois hagiois, Sancta sanctis*" (God's holy gifts for God's holy people)! "The faithful (*sancti*) are fed by Christ's holy body and blood (*sancta*) to grow in the communion (*koinonia*) of the Holy Spirit and to communicate it to the world" (CCC 948).

Let us begin with the second meaning, communion among holy persons. This is the meaning people usually think of when they are talking about the "communion of saints".[2] "Communion of saints" means first of all that there is a *communion of life* between *all* who belong to Christ, between *all* the members of his Body. As the Council says:

> When the Lord comes in glory, and all his angels with him [cf. Mt 25:31], death will be no more and all things will be subject to him [cf. 1 Cor 15:26–27]. But in the present time some of his disciples are pilgrims on earth. Others have died and are being purified, while still others are in glory, contemplating, "in full light, God himself triune and one, exactly as he is."[3]

The Church does not come to an end at the threshold of death. She is the communion of *all* who live in Christ. Awareness of the unity of the earthly with the heavenly

---

[2] Cf. H. de Lubac, "*Sanctorum communio*", in *Theological Fragments* (San Francisco: Ignatius Press, 1989), 17–18.

[3] LG 49; cf. CCC 954.

Church has all too often been weakened in our own time. And yet this is an *essential* dimension of the Church. When we live with full consciousness in this communion with those who have been perfected in Christ, our sense of the Church attains a quite different breadth and confidence than when it is restricted to those who are alive on earth here and now. "We are all Church"—that is a "slogan" of a protest movement in my home country. Yes, it is true, but only if "*we . . . all*" really includes *all* who belong to Christ, both on this side and on the other side of the frontier of death. It is a frightful impoverishment, in fact mutilation, of the Church when she is seen as no more than the "we" who are visibly assembled here and now. Is it not, by contrast, the Church's glory, her inexhaustible vitality, that in the *communio sanctorum* we can *all* reach out our hands to one another, can exist for one another, beyond all the limitations of time and space? Those who lived and believed before us are no less Church than those of us alive today. We cannot stress enough how real our communion with them with is. As the Council says:

All . . . who are of Christ and who have his Spirit form one Church and in Christ cleave together. So it is that the union of the wayfarers with the brethren who sleep in the peace of Christ is in no way interrupted, but on the contrary, according to the constant faith of the Church, this union is reinforced by an exchange of spiritual goods. *Being more closely united to Christ, those who dwell in heaven* fix the whole Church more firmly in holiness, raise up the dignity of the divine worship she offers God on earth, and help in many different ways to the building up of the

Church. . . . So by their fraternal concern is our weakness greatly helped.[4]

Again, we cannot stress enough how realistically this has to be taken. Those who have been perfected in Christ, the saints in heaven, are *more profoundly united with Christ* than they were on earth. Surely, then, their whole being must be incorporated into Jesus' "being for us". The help we receive from heaven—our "*richest* help", says the Council—is like an invisible yet mighty river of life. Saint Thérèse knew about this and spoke of it with boldness: "If God grants my wishes, my heaven will take place on earth to the end of time. Yes, I want to spend my heaven doing good on earth."[5] At the end of her life, someone said to her: " 'You'll *look down* on us from heaven, won't you?' She replied spontaneously: 'No. I'll *come* down!' "[6]

What Thérèse says here so unaffectedly corresponds to the Apostle's vision on Patmos. The angel showed him "the holy city Jerusalem coming down out of heaven from God" (Rev 21:10−11). What Thérèse says of herself is true of the whole Church in heaven: she is wholly united with Christ, but she is also the one who is to come with him. The Apocalypse calls our Lord him "who is to come" (cf. Rev 1:4). So, then, heaven, too, comes with him on earth. There is another bold assertion of Saint Thérèse's: "In heaven God *must* fulfill my desires, because I have never done my own will on earth."[7] Mary

[4] LG 49; cf. CCC 954−56.
[5] *Derniers entretiens*, July 17, 1897.
[6] Ibid., September 26, 1897.
[7] Ibid., July 13, 1897, no. 2.

did only God's will on earth, and so she is "for that reason the most active saint in heaven."[8] The *communio sanctorum* means that heaven is close to earth, that Jesus' words, "I am with you always", include all those he has brought home to the Father: "Here am I, and the children God has given me" (Heb 2:13). He is always with us *all*, with all who are with him.

How does this helping closeness of the saints in heaven affect the Church? Should she not be making constant progress? Should she not be ever more triumphant, strengthened as she is by an ever greater company of the saints? Should the Church not be visibly and clearly blossoming beneath this mighty protection from above? Is the *communio sanctorum* not proving itself to be powerless, even a pious deception?

We must ask ourselves a counterquestion. What do we expect of the saints in heaven, these brothers and sisters of ours who are already perfected and yet full of love and concern for us? That through their activity all adversities be done away with, that the Church may enjoy the splendor of recognition on all sides? Do we not these days often expect more of the Church than her own real life? What she really has to communicate is divine adoption, grace, "living union" with Christ. Are not these very things overlooked, even within the Church, as unimportant, while at the same time people have other expectations of the Church that she is bound to disappoint,[9] for

---

[8] Balthasar, *Homo creatus est*, 163.
[9] Cf. J. Ratzinger, *Auf Christus schauen* (Freiburg: Herder, 1989), 79.

example, that she should offer an "ideal *world*", in which everything, from the protection of the environment and human relationships to the Church's own public reputation, is "just fine"?

The Church, with her institutions and sacraments, is part of *this* world, this present age, and with the world she "sighs and groans". Time and again she disappoints purely human expectations. And so it is that people turn away from the Church, indignant and incensed because she is not the "ideal society" they had expected. Is not the source of the great apostasy in our rich countries the fact that the *communio sanctorum* is no longer valued, too little proclaimed, as the Church's real treasure?

The growth, the help, given us from heaven comes about through communion in *heavenly* goods. The communion of the saints in Christ grows through communion in the holy gifts, the *sancta*. Nowhere is this clearer than in the celebration of the Eucharist, in which Christ is at once both the Gift and the Giver: "For participation in the Body and Blood of Christ has no other effect than this, that we pass over into that which we receive."[10] In the celebration of Mass, heaven and earth, heavenly Church and pilgrim Church, are gathered together. Is it often and clearly enough proclaimed that we *really do* celebrate the Eucharist "with all the angels and saints"? "Without their presence, no Eucharist is celebrated on earth."[11] In the "Communicantes" of the Roman Canon,

---

[10] St. Leo the Great, cited in LG 26.
[11] Balthasar, *Homo creatus est*, 156.

and then again in the "Nobis quoque peccatoribus", we unite ourselves "above all with the glorious Ever-Virgin Mary, Mother of our God and Lord Jesus Christ", with Saint Joseph and the apostles, martyrs, and all the saints. In communion with them we celebrate Mass. The *communio sanctorum* is expressed in a particularly impressive way in the prayer, "Supplices te rogamus": "We humbly beseech thee, almighty God, bid this sacrifice to be brought by the hands of thy holy angel to thine altar on high, in the presence of thy divine majesty, that as many of us as partake from this altar of the sacred Body and Blood of thy Son may be *filled with all heavenly benediction and grace.*" This, too, must be understood literally and realistically: When we receive from the *one* altar, the one altar of heaven and earth, the *one* Gift, Christ's Body and Blood, we really are filled "omni benedictione coelesti et gratia" (with all heavenly benediction and grace).

The *communio sanctorum* is the communion of all those who, like Christ and with Christ, "*stand in*" *for one another*. The Church as the *communio sanctorum* is, then, not just one special interest group among many. No, she is the center of mankind, "the heart of the world". Again we need to understand in a very realistic way what we pray in one of the prayers of the Missal: "As often as the sacrifice of the Cross, by which 'Christ our Pasch has been sacrificed' (cf. 1 Cor 5:7), is celebrated on the altar, the work of our redemption is carried out."[12] In the inconspicuous, humble outward form of the celebration

---

[12] LG 3; CCC 1364.

of Mass, "the work of our redemption is carried out": "May this sacrifice of our reconciliation advance, we beseech thee, O Lord, the peace and salvation *of the whole world*."[13] Only in heaven will we see how we owe our salvation to the *communio sanctorum*. Saint Thérèse puts it very vividly: "In heaven we shall meet no indifferent glances, because all the elect will realize that they owe one another the graces that brought them the crown of life."[14]

The *communio sanctorum* is the "boundless communion of those who stand in for one another".[15] *Here* lies its immeasurable efficacy for the salvation of "the whole world". "One for the other": that is the life principle of the *communio sanctorum* as it comes to us from Christ. It also shows its efficacy in a special way in our communion with *the departed*. "Our prayer for them is capable not only of helping them, but also of making their intercession for us effective" (CCC 958). "[T]he least of our acts done in charity redounds to the *profit of all*. Every sin harms this communion" (CCC 953). The *communio sanctorum* means that we bear responsibility for one another, *all for one another*. No man is an island. "None of us lives to himself, and none of us dies to himself" (Rom 14:7). In the words of Léon Bloy, the *communio sanctorum* is the "antidote and counteraction to the scattering of Babel".[16]

---

[13] Eucharistic Prayer III.

[14] *Derniers entretiens*, July 15, 1897, no. 5.

[15] Balthasar, *Homo creatus est*, 156.

[16] "Antidote et contrepartie de la Dispersion de Babel" (*Le pèlerin de l'Absolu*, 377).

And again Thérèse in the *Derniers entretiens*: "What will it be like in heaven when souls recognize those who have saved them?"[17]

PRAISED BE JESUS CHRIST!

[17] "Qu'est-ce que ce sera donc au Ciel quand les âmes connaîtront celles qui les auront sauvées?!" (August 23, 1897, no. 6).

FIFTH DAY

Third Meditation
"Tertio Millennio Adveniente"

Holy Father, dear brothers in the Lord,

"The Church will be perfected in glory only at the end of time." She has not yet been perfected. Only then will she be perfected. "*Gloriose* consummabitur": she will be perfected in glory! In other words, she has not yet been perfected *in glory*. In a certain sense, she has already been perfected, but not yet in glory. *How*, then, is she already perfected, and what does she still lack for her to be perfected in *glory*? Her Lord and Master was perfected through his Passion and Cross. And when is the Church's final perfecting to be? "At the end of time". She will soon have been waiting for two thousand years, and even though "with the Lord one day is as a thousand years" (2 Pet 3:8), we cannot fail to ask whether we still have to wait longer for the final perfection. It is already a long time in coming, too long, all too long, one is tempted to say, especially since our Lord in many of his words has given us the hope that his coming is imminent, and prophetic words have confirmed it (cf. Mk 9:1; Rev 22:20).

Now, as the second millennium since the birth of Christ draws to a close, the question becomes all the more urgent: How far has the Church got on her journey through time? "Custos, quid de nocte?" Is the night far gone? Is day about to dawn?

What the Church as a whole lives out and suffers is mirrored in the life of the individual. Each of us must ask himself: When will our earthly pilgrimage come to an end? But each of us must also ask: How have I travelled on my own personal journey of faith? "Nox praecessit, dies autem appropinquabit", (The night is far gone, the day is at hand) (Rom 13:12). How far has our night gone? Let us devote these last two meditations of our retreat to the "Last Things" of the Church and of our own life, with special reference to the approaching *Great Jubilee*. May the Lord, through his Holy Spirit, enable us to recognize "the signs of the times"! "The end of the ages has already come upon us (cf. 1 Cor 10:11), and the world's renewal is irrevocably established and, in a certain sense, is really anticipated in this age. For the Church on earth is even now marked by a true, albeit imperfect holiness" (LG 48).

The only *new* age is the time *post Christum natum* (since the birth of Christ). Since Good Friday and the cry "It is finished" (Jn 19:30), since Easter Sunday morning, since the day of Pentecost, "the world's renewal is already irrevocably established." The hope for a New Pentecost in the Church, which is associated with the Second Vatican Council, is not a hope for some *new* age of history but the hope that Christ be more deeply known and loved, of which the Church at the Council makes this confession: "[T]he key, the center, and the purpose of the whole of man's history is to be found in its Lord and Master."[1]

What is true of the Church is true also of the individual: "We are called children of God, and so we *are*" (1 Jn 3:1). "You *have been* raised with Christ" (Col 3:1). But "it does not yet appear what we *shall* be" (1 Jn 3:2). When will it appear? When will the perfection come *perfectly*? Are we not at the threshold of a new period in the life of the Church, a new outpouring of the Holy Spirit?

The *temptation* to dream of a "golden age" of faith has accompanied the Church throughout the centuries. Now, as we look toward the year 2000, it is tempting to hope for a new epoch of faith, a time in which the Church will shine forth, opposition die away, and the faith be triumphant. We in the West used to focus that hope on the persecuted Christians of the East. While secularization was emptying churches in the West, we expected a great upsurge of purified faith from the Church in the East. "Ex occidente luxus, ex oriente lux!" Meanwhile, we have to admit that, while the path of the Church in the East is indeed different from what it was under Communism, it is no less arduous: the devastation left behind by Communism is too deep. And in the Third World, too, there are no signs of a "new age" for the Church. Now as before, large parts of Asia are unwelcoming territory for the Christian faith, and in Latin America the Church is going through a deep testing at the hands of the sects. It seems as if, at the end of this millennium,

---

[1] GS 10; CCC 450; John Paul II, apostolic letter *Tertio millennio adveniente* (November 10, 1994), no. 59 (hereafter abbreviated TMA).

the torments of the Church are increasing. And is not the Church's situation mirrored in the life of the individual, in our own personal journey of faith? Have our great hopes for a great breakthrough in faith, for a "successful Christian existence", been fulfilled? Is it not our lot, day after day, to continue the often humiliating struggle against our own imperfection and the power of the Evil One?

These sober observations have nothing to do with pessimism. They merely indicate the situation of the Church and the individual believer in the "age of the Church". Saint Augustine's words did apply and do apply to *all* the eras of the Church's history between Pentecost and the Parousia: "[T]he Church progresses on her pilgrimage amidst this world's persecutions and God's consolations."[2] She never lacks either God's consolations nor the torments of the world. There was a time after the Council when it was frowned upon to speak of the world as the "vale of tears". And yet how consoling it is, "gementes et flentes in hac lacrimarum valle" (mourning and weeping in this vale of tears), to greet Mary, our "advocata" (advocate), "spes nostra" (our hope), and seek refuge under her protection ("sub tuum praesidium confugimus")! The Church's way will always be a *pilgrimage*. Let us never forget that here on earth we are "aliens and exiles" (1 Pet 2:11), with no permanent rights of citizenship. (In Switzerland they would say we have the status of *saisoniers*, migrant workers.) And if we do forget this,

---

[2] *De civitate Dei* 18, 51; CCC 769.

if we prefer not to admit it, because we have "settled down", then "the world" reminds us by persecuting us or treating as "aliens".

The word "parish" (*parochia*) means a community of *paroikoi*, of aliens without the right of domicile. That is why the Church can never identify herself with *one* people, *one* race, *one* nation. As the Epistle to Diognetus says, for Christians "*every* homeland is a foreign country, and every foreign country is a homeland." It is not only persecution that imposes on us this life as a stranger and pilgrim. It is also often a conscious choice in imitation of Christ, who "came to his own home, and his own people received him not" (Jn 1:11). "Foxes have holes, and birds of the air have nests; but the Son of man has nowhere to lay his head" (Mt 8:20). This is the *conditio christiana*: as poor to follow the poor Christ, to have one's home in heaven, and to be a pilgrim on earth. There are certain texts of Scripture that today we prefer to ignore. For example: "Do not love the world or the things in the world! . . . The world passes away, and the lust of it." (1 Jn 2:15, 17). Perhaps such words were too quickly dismissed as "flight from the world". Today we need them.

Now the astonishing thing is this: the men who so ardently yearned for their eternal homeland, who spoke of the *fuga mundi*, were great men of civilization and culture, devoted collectors and transmitters of everything beautiful, true, and good. The ideologies, which tried to impose by violence a new humanity, a paradise on earth, left behind total destruction and devastation. (Horrific reports have come to us in the last few days of the extent of the genocide in Cambodia, planned and carried out by

Pol Pot.) By contrast, Christian monasticism, which also dreams of a new humanity, but one that will be perfected only in the world to come, does not devastate and destroy but preserves, cultivates, builds up. Is it not strange that Christendom's great cultural achievements were the work of men who said in the same breath, "Media vita in morte sumus" (in the midst of life we are in death), and who sighed, "post hoc exilium" (after this our exile), to behold the glory of heaven?

The builders of our cathedrals knew that they would not see the completion of their work. Where did men with such a strong sense of being pilgrims find the *patience* to begin such works? The answer is perhaps as follows: The man who knows he is a pilgrim does not have to, does not want to, possess and enjoy everything in this vale of tears. He regards himself as one link in a long chain of predecessors and successors. For the sake of the greater, common work, he is ready to make sacrifices. Such men were intensely aware that "here we have no lasting city, but we seek the city which is to come" (Heb 13:14), and yet they summoned up the patience to build cathedrals over the course of the generations.

There is a great temptation to hope that one day there might be a time when the Church on earth will no longer carry the yoke of pilgrimage. But the yoke will not be taken from her shoulders. It will only be made *lighter* for her, because it is *his* yoke: "Take *my* yoke upon you . . . for my yoke is easy, and my burden is light" (Mt 11:29–30). But it remains a yoke to be carried.

Until our Lord comes again, the Church, all of us her members, will only be "guests upon earth". But this does not mean that the Church has no interest in this earth of ours. *Pilgrims* are not *vandals*. The great virtue of pilgrimage is *patience, perseverance*. How patiently the Church does her work in education, in the service of the sick and the poor! The exhortations of Saint Paul are testimonies to this patience. We do not see here an impatient apocalyptic prophet waiting for God to intervene and solve all problems. No, here speaks a man who draws from faith the patience of hope, which does good with perseverance.

The new evangelization will probably not be dissimilar to the first evangelization. It was the small cells of Christian communities and homes that proclaimed *by their life* the "gospel of life" and gave back a *taste for life* to the morally dissolute society of antiquity. With how much *patience*—and not without the mighty assistance of grace —were the seeds of the virtues planted in a "heartless [and] ruthless" world (Rom 1:31), so that something like a "civilization of love" could begin to grow! And yet so much that was unredeemed, unevangelized, remained in the intense early period of Christianity. *Tertio millennio adveniente* mentions as an example the strange blindness to slavery and torture, for which the Church today should repent (cf. TMA 35). And there is so much that is unredeemed, unevangelized, or rather that needs to be evangelized anew, in the Church of our time, in our own lives! The words of the Council apply to the *whole* time of the Church's pilgrimage: "Christ, 'holy, innocent, and undefiled' [Heb 7:26], knew nothing of sin [cf. 2 Cor 5:21], but came only to expiate the sins of the people [cf. Heb 2:17]. The Church, however, clasping sinners to her bosom, at once holy and *always* in need of purification, follows *constantly* the path of penance and renewal."[3] As long as her pilgrimage lasts, the Church is *semper purificanda*, ever to be purified. She constantly needs penance and renewal. As long as the Church is a pilgrim on earth, as long as all things have not yet been "subjected" to Christ (cf. 1 Cor 15:28), the Church's salvation, the salvation of each one of us, has indeed already been accomplished by Christ but is not yet *perfected* in us: "Christ, having been offered once to bear the sins of many, will appear a second time, not to deal with sin but *to save* those who are eagerly waiting for him" (Heb 9:28).

Even our noblest endeavors, even our most Christian concerns, require purification, redemption. To conclude, I mention just *one* concern that the Holy Father urgently brings to the attention of the Church and all Christians: the desire for the unity of Christians. The Council said that the ruptures between Christians did not occur "without human sin on both sides".[4] It has become clearer to us today that a separated Christendom is also a sign of how much there is in the history of Christians that is unredeemed, in need of healing and salvation. Today, when the endeavors for Christian unity are evident throughout the world, we must also ask ourselves whether the quest for unity is not also *semper purificanda*.

One of the great spiritual masters of our time, the Coptic Orthodox monk Father *Matta El-Maskine* (Matthew the Poor Man), draws our attention to the fact that not only the divisions but also the efforts for unity can be

[3] LG 8; CCC 827.

[4] Decree on Ecumenism *Unitatis redintegratio* (November 21, 1964), no. 3; CCC 817.

marked by the spirit of the world. Are they concerned with that unity for which Jesus prayed, "that they may all be one . . . *in us* . . ." (Jn 17:21), "even as thou, Father, art in me, and I in thee" (Jn 17:21)? Or are they interested in coalitions, in a "unity that makes for strength"? *Amba Matta* asks whether striving for unity can involve the temptation to throw off the yoke of weakness, so that we can be strong in the face of the world. A Church that has been persecuted for centuries, as the Coptic Church has been, can recognize this temptation.[5] But is it not also there in the midst of the efforts of the "Great Sister Churches"? Might it not be that our Lord is allowing us to carry the cross, the shame, of disunity, to the derision and outrage of the world, because we are not yet in a position to live in unity in the way that the Father and the Son are one? Does the Church not triumph precisely when she is "weak", when she is led by "the Lamb, standing as though it had been slain"? In her novel *Die Magdeburgische Hochzeit*, which deals with the divisions between Christians in Germany, Gertrud von Le Fort puts these words into the mouth of the Catholic Field Marshal Tilly as he speaks to a young Protestant officer: "*Mary triumphs with the sword, not in her hand, but in her heart.*"

PRAISED BE JESUS CHRIST!

---

[5] Matta El-Maskine, *Prière, Esprit Saint et 'Unité chrétienne* (Begrolles-en-Mauges: Abbaye de Bellefontaine, 1990), 155.

Fourth Meditation
"Rise Up to Meet the Bridegroom!"

> But at midnight there was a cry, "Behold, the bridegroom! Come out to meet him!" (Mt 25:6).

The Church, says the Council, "constitutes the seed and beginning of this Kingdom [of Christ] on earth. As she gradually grows, she strains toward the perfection of the Kingdom, and with all her powers she hopes and yearns to be united with her King in glory" (LG 5). The Church is a living communion with Jesus Christ. How could the Church not be yearning to be united with Christ? The final goal of the Church, her perfection in Christ, will be the theme of this last meditation. We shall look at three aspects of it, which at first sight are quite different from each other. What is common is the longing for Christ that defines them:

—Liturgical prayer toward the east, *versus orientem*;

—Pastoral ministry as an expression of love for Christ;

—The final testing of the Church.

1. The early Christian liturgy was filled with the longing for the coming of the Lord: "*Marana tha*, Our Lord, come!" (1 Cor 16:22). That is the liturgical cry of the Church, which "the Spirit and the Bride" (Rev 22:17)

call out to Christ and to which he replies: "Surely I am coming soon" (Rev 22:20). The celebration of the Eucharist is the privileged place for the Church to utter her "*Marana tha*". Here, in our Lord's sacramental presence, we are given the "*pignus futurae gloriae*" (pledge of the glory to come) (cf. CCC 1402). Is this *eschatological orientation* of our prayer and worship established with sufficient clarity in the minds of the faithful, in preaching, in liturgical practice? The chief issue is the *interior* orientation of liturgical prayer. The exterior form—for example, the direction in which the celebration takes place— is important only in second place. As Cardinal Ratzinger has said: "There is only one inner direction of the Eucharist, namely, from Christ in the Holy Spirit to the Father. The only question is how this can be best expressed in liturgical form."[1]

How is this expressed in the language of liturgical gesture? Before the reform of the liturgy, it was the usual practice for priest and people in common to direct their prayer to the Father "per Christum Dominum nostrum". It was not a question of the priest's turning away from the people but of their common turning toward the Lord. "Conversi ad Dominum oremus" (Turned to the Lord, let us pray), Saint Augustine usually says at the end of his sermons.

The *eschatological* component is emphasized by the *eastward direction*, the "orient-ation", of Christian prayer. From earliest times Christians prayed privately and pub-

---

[1] J. Ratzinger, *The Feast of Faith*, trans. Graham Harrison (San Francisco: Ignatius Press, 1986), 140.

licly *versus orientem*, toward the East, in ardent expectation of the Second Coming of our Lord. Numerous works of scholarly research on the location of the axis in medieval churches have shown how deep-seated this sense of the East was. Saint Stephen's Cathedral in Vienna was aligned, at its axis, with the rising sun on Saint Stephen's Day, 1137, the day its foundations were laid. Christ, the "Oriens ex alto" (the Dayspring from on high), shines forth in the splendor of his saints.

How impressive it is, even today, when the morning light pours through the east doors or windows of Saint Peter's! From the beginning, the Holy Father has celebrated here *versus orientem* (toward the east), toward Christ, *obviam Sponso* (facing the Bridegroom). The inclusion of this cosmic symbolism in the liturgy has become largely alien to us today. And yet how important such signs are for "incarnating" the faith. The common prayer of priest and faithful *versus orientem* connected this cosmic "orientation" with faith in the Resurrection of Christ, the *sol oriens*, the Rising Sun, and with his *Parousia* in glory.

True, this liturgical symbolism should not be absolutized, nor should it become an ideological point of contention. *One* aspect of it, though, is unreservedly valid and necessary: common liturgical prayer is *obviam Sponso*, a meeting with the Bridegroom, an anticipation of Christ's final coming. It is *he* who must stand at the center. *His* death and *his* Resurrection we confess, and for *his* return we hope.

Historically speaking, celebration *versus populum*, toward the people, is a *new* form of celebration. It is no less legitimate, as long as the focus on Christ remains clear, when, for example, the altar, which is "the symbol of Christ himself" (CCC 1383), is truly at the center of the liturgy, and when the priest, who stands at the altar *in persona Christi capitis*, is totally "relativized" toward Christ, when he points toward *Christ*, in the attitude of John the Baptist: "He must increase, but I must decrease" (Jn 3:30). Being a "friend of the Bridegroom", rejoicing at "the voice of the Bridegroom"—that is the right attitude of the priest, whose ministry becomes for the faithful an invitation: "*Obviam Sponso!*" (Let us go out to meet the Bridegroom!).

2. The longing to go to meet Christ also means the desire to be "conformed" to him (cf. Rom 8:29). *Obviam Sponso* means not just hoping for his *Parousia* but first and foremost going out to meet him in the place to which he descended: even death on the Cross (cf. Phil 2:8). A sermon of Saint Augustine's on the Transfiguration of our Lord speaks vividly of this following of Christ:

> Peter did not yet understand this when he wanted to remain with Christ on the mountain. It has been reserved for you, Peter, but for after death. For now, Jesus says: "Go down to toil on earth, to serve on earth, to be scorned and crucified on earth. Life goes down to be killed; Bread goes down to suffer hunger; the Way goes down to be exhausted on his journey; the Spring goes down to suffer thirst; and you refuse to suffer?"[2]

Obviam Sponso! That also means going out to meet Christ with the burning lamps of pastoral charity, *amor*

---

[2] St. Augustine, *Sermo* 78, 6; CCC 556.

pastoralis. "The Lord said clearly that concern for his flock was proof of love for him."[3] "The priest is called to be the living image of Jesus Christ, the Bridegroom of the Church" (PDV 22). "The inner principle, the power animating and directing the spiritual life of the priest, insofar as he is conformed to Christ, the Head and Shepherd, is *pastoral charity*, as a participation in Christ's own pastoral charity" (PDV 23). *Obviam Sponso!* For us priests, that means: more and more loving the Church, the flock entrusted to us, with the love with which he "loved the church and gave himself up for her" (Eph 5:25).

3. *Obviam Sponso* also means, for the Church as a whole, for the Bride of Christ, being *conformed to Christ* more and more. She, too, like him, like each of the faithful, "through many tribulations must enter the kingdom of God" (Acts 14:22). As we look toward the *Great Jubilee*, this question confronts the Church with new clarity: In the presence of the great, the vast number of martyrs of our century, whose names are written in the Book of Life, we hear anew the urgent cry of "the souls of those who had been slain for the word of God and for the witness they had borne . . . 'O Sovereign Lord, holy and true, how long before thou wilt judge . . . ?' Then they were . . . told to rest a *little longer*, until the number of their fellow servants and their brethren should be complete, who were to be killed as they themselves had been" (Rev 6:9–11). What is this "little longer", this "short time" (*chronon mikron*) of waiting, of resting? It is the "time of

---

[3] St. John Chrysostom, *De sacerdotio* 2, 4; CCC 1551.

the Church". We reflected on its significance yesterday.
Now let me make three complementary points:

a. It is the time of waiting, of enduring "to the end"
(Mt 10:22). According to a profound idea of *Origen*, it
is the waiting not only of the pilgrim Church but of the
whole Church of heaven and earth. The saints of heaven
are also waiting with us. They wait until *all* the members
of the Body of Christ, to the very last, have been saved
and fulfilled.[4] The *whole* Church is in an "intermediate
state". She waits to be united with her Bridegroom, and
all of her members, each in his own way, has a share in
this "active waiting": the saints of heaven through their
intercession, their protection of us pilgrims; the Pilgrim
Church through our completing in our earthly life "what
is lacking in Christ's afflictions for the sake of his Body,
that is, the church" (Col 1:24). Only with the resurrection
"at the last day" (CCC 1001) will the "building up [of]
the body of Christ" (Eph 4:12) be complete. This view
of the Church in *solidarity* in the "intermediate state" can
help us to overcome a "soteriological individualism".

b. It is the time of the final trials of the Church. The
Catechism says of these:

> Before Christ's second coming, the Church must pass
> through a final trial that will shake the faith of many be-
> lievers. The persecution that accompanies her pilgrimage
> on earth will unveil the "mystery of iniquity" in the form
> of a religious deception offering men an apparent solution
> to their problems at the price of apostasy from the truth.

[4] *Homily 7 on Leviticus*, cited in H. de Lubac, *Catholicism* trans.
Lancelot C. Sheppard and Sr. Elizabeth Englund, O.C.D. (San Francisco: Ignatius Press, 1988), text 23.

> The supreme religious deception is that of the Antichrist, a pseudo-messianism by which man glorifies himself in place of God and of his Messiah come in the flesh (CCC 675).

Where do we stand today? We know neither the day nor the hour (cf. Mk 13:32). But this we do know: "It is full time now for you to wake from sleep. For salvation is *nearer* to us *now* than when we first believed" (Rom 13:11). We do not know *how* near the day is, but we do have this belief: "The Church will enter the glory of the kingdom only through this final Passover, when she will follow her Lord in his death and Resurrection. *The kingdom will be fulfilled, then, not by a historic triumph of the Church through a progressive ascendancy,* but only by God's victory over the final unleashing of evil, which will cause his Bride to come down from heaven" (CCC 677).

Obviam Sponso! The way by which the Church goes out to meet Christ is the "narrow way of the Cross".[5]

c. The coming of Christ in glory will be his own free and sovereign deed. And yet the way of the Church, as she goes out to meet her Bridegroom, is connected with *a special mystery* that we have already considered several times in these exercises.

> The glorious Messiah's coming is suspended at every moment of history until his recognition by "all Israel" [Rom 11:26], for "a hardening has come upon part of Israel" [v. 25] in their "unbelief" toward Jesus [v. 20]. . . . "For if their rejection means the reconciliation of the world, what will their acceptance mean but life from the dead?"

[5] AG 1; CCC 853.

[v. 15]. The "full inclusion" [v. 12] of the Jews in the Messiah's salvation, in the wake of "the full number of the Gentiles" [v. 25], will enable the People of God to achieve "the measure of the stature of the fullness of Christ" [Eph 4:13], in which God "may be all in all" [1 Cor 15:28] (CCC 674).

Will this "time for establishing all" (Acts 3:21) fall *within* history? Will it be the end of history? *One* thing is certain for us in faith: the way of the Church *obviam Sponso* is inseparably connected with the mystery of Israel. The "times of the Gentiles" (Lk 21:24) are still going on, and still a large part of Israel is waiting for the Messiah. All our endeavors in the cause of Christian unity are important, indeed an urging of the Holy Spirit. And yet, as long as the Church is on pilgrimage, as long as the "meantime" between the first and second comings of our Lord continues, so the Church remains unfulfilled and her unity fragmentary. That is why she yearns to be united with her Spouse, with him whom Simeon praised in the Temple as "a light for revelation to the Gentiles, and for glory to thy people Israel" (Lk 2:32).

PRAISED BE JESUS CHRIST!

CONCLUDING MEDITATION

"IN THE HEART OF THE CHURCH
I WILL BE LOVE!"

Holy Father, dear brothers in the Lord,

Pope Paul VI once called the Church "the visible plan of God's love for humanity".[1] It is to this *plan of God's love* that our meditations have been devoted during these spiritual exercises. "God [is] infinitely perfect and blessed in himself" (CCC 1). With this first sentence of the Catechism we began our retreat. We followed the various stages of the way by which the infinitely perfect and blessed triune God gives men, his creatures, a share in his own blessedness by calling them together in his family, *the Church* (cf. CCC 1).

In our meditations on the Church, that great "plan of God's love", we followed the Second Vatican Council: "During the Council, the Church, precisely out of a desire to be fully faithful to her Master, questioned herself about her own identity, and discovered anew the depth of her mystery as the Body and Bride of Christ (TMA 19)." At the same time, we have been guided by a concern with where the Church stands *today*, at the threshold of the third millennium *post Christum natum*. "Custos, quid de nocte?" "When the Son of man comes, will he find faith on earth?" (Lk 18:8)—or is salvation "nearer

---

[1] Address of June 22, 1973; CCC 776.

now than when first we believed" (Rom 13:11)? Are we entering more deeply into the night, into darkness? Or is it now full time "to wake from sleep. . . . Nox praecessit, dies autem appropinquavit" (Rom 13:11–12)? We know neither the day nor the hour (cf. Mk 13:32), only that we should stay awake (cf. Mt 24:37). And we know with the unshakeable certainty of faith (cf. CCC 157) that "*already* the final age of the world *is with us*, and the renewal of the world is irrevocably under way; it is even now anticipated in a certain real way."[2]

On what is this certainty grounded? To what signs can we point to show that the claim is in a certain sense reasonable? The Council gives this reason: "For the Church on earth is endowed already with a sanctity that is real but imperfect."[3] And at the beginning of the fifth chapter of the Dogmatic Constitution on the Church, we read: "The Church . . . is held, as a matter of faith, to be *unfailingly* holy."[4] This *Holy Church* is "the plan of God's love". She is the beloved Bride, for whom Christ gave himself up, in order to *sanctify* her. If the Church means "living union with Christ", then she can only be *holy* as he is holy, and *sanctifying* through him. By faith we are certain that the Church will never be lacking in holiness, even if her members in a large part are sinners. The man who finds the Church's *holiness* has discovered "the depths of her mystery". To see it is the joy of God and the "longing of the angels" (cf. 1 Pet 1:12). Our final meditation will be devoted to the Church as *holy*, so that our love

[2] LG 48; CCC 670.
[3] Ibid.
[4] LG 39; CCC 823.

for the Church may be enkindled by Christ's love for his Bride.

In our opening meditation we followed in the footsteps of the first disciples of Jesus when they first encountered the Master. In our concluding meditation let us again follow the disciples, this time to Jerusalem, to the Temple. And again our Lord invites them *to see*. It is as if, just before his Passion, he wants to show them once more what is most important. It is as if he is again saying to them: "Come and see" (Jn 1:39). And yet what he shows them is surprisingly "little", surprisingly "slight":

> And he sat down opposite the treasury, and watched the multitude putting money into the treasury. Many rich people put in large sums. And a poor widow came, and put in two copper coins, which make a penny. And he called his disciples to him, and said to them, "Truly, I say to you, this poor widow has put in more than all those who are contributing to the treasury. For they all contributed out of their abundance; but she out of her poverty has put in everything she had, her whole living (*holon* ton bion autēs)" (Mk 12:41–44).

In Mark as in Luke, this episode forms the conclusion and climax of the words and deeds of Jesus, immediately before the eschatological discourse and the Passion narrative. In this little scene the whole Gospel is again summed up. It is a kind of abridgment of the Gospel.

First of all, there is the gaze of Jesus. Jesus sits and *sees* how the multitude throw money into the treasury. We could meditate at length on this *looking of our Lord*. For how are we supposed to become his disciples if we do not become familiar with *his gaze*, if *his way of see-ing* does not become ours? He teaches his disciples *to see* things, situations, people *with his eyes: that is how Jesus forms his Church*. Seeing with his eyes, understanding with his mind, willing with his will, feeling with his Heart—from this springs the Church, this is the secret of her holi-ness.

Jesus looks at the multitude of men and sees many rich people throwing large sums into the treasury. And then Jesus *sees* a *poor widow*. Two copper coins are all she throws in. *Now* Jesus calls his disciples together: "*convocans*", says the Vulgate. *Convocatio* is a name of the Church. He calls them together in order to show them the poor widow. He says a great thing about this poor woman: She has given more than all the rest; she has given her *all*, "holon ton bion autēs", *all* that she had for life, "her whole life". It is because of *this* poor woman that our Lord calls his disciples together, as if he had something very important to show, something particularly remarkable.

The widow does not notice that she has been seen, that *he* has seen her. He says nothing to *her*, no praise, no promise of reward. All the more purely does her unob-trusive action shine, unobserved by the wealthy, by the crowd of people in the Temple, unobserved, too, by the disciples, who—as so often!—would have noticed noth-ing had the Master not pointed it out to them. The ac-tion of the widow is beautiful, because it is completely *unselfconscious*. Here the left hand does not know what the right is doing (cf. Mt 6:3). Here alms are not given "in order to be praised by men" (Mt 6:2). And this action is done in earnest, in complete earnest, because the widow gave away *all* that she had to live on.

Why does our Lord call the disciples together to show them this poor widow? Because they must *learn* to *see* people like this poor widow. The disciples, the pastors, must have an eye for these people, and so Jesus calls them to *himself*, so that they can learn to see from his "angle". And they must learn to be amazed at *this* kind of greatness: they must learn to see who is *great* in the Kingdom of Heaven. Jesus shapes their gaze, so that they can become shepherds after his own Heart.

Shortly before his Passion, Jesus shows his disciples, as in a mirror image, the whole meaning of his own mission, for he came in poverty, he emptied himself (cf. Phil 2:7), made himself the servant of all, and finally threw "his whole life" for us into the Temple treasury of the Father. This poor widow is a pure and genuine image of Jesus himself, and it is no surprise that patristic exegesis sees in her a figure of the Church, who "understands that even her very living is not of her own desert, but of divine grace".[5]

When we pose the question of the Church's "identity" (cf. TMA 19), we are referred to this figure of the poor widow. Our Lord summons us who have been called to the apostolic ministry. He calls us together, to himself, and shows us this figure of the Church, whom we so easily overlook but who is great in his eyes, the poor, un-

[5] St. Bede the Venerable, *In Luc.*, cap. 86, cited by St. Thomas Aquinas, *Catena aurea: Commentary on the Four Gospels*, vol. 2, *St. Mark*, trans. J. D. Dalgairns (Oxford: J. H. Parker, 1842), 253.

noticed figure of unselfconscious, selfless devotion. He
shows us where *Holy Church* is to be found and invites us
to share his *love* for this "poor widow Church", to join in
his jubilation and joy that it has pleased the Father to let
his mystery shine forth in these "babes" (Mt 11:25). *That*
is the "depth of the mystery of the Church as Body and
Bride of Christ", which the Council rediscovered (TMA
19). The Church will never lack this true and hidden holiness. May we pastors never lack the eyes of Jesus for
seeing it and for praising the Father, the Lord of heaven
and earth, for it (cf. Mt 11:25)! Our Lord himself helps
us in this task by putting men on the Church's path who
see with his eyes, who feel and think with his Heart. Our
Lord gives us luminous figures that make the holiness of
the Church visible.

In the *Catechism of the Catholic Church*, we are given
a great number of the testimonies and teachings of the
saints, both men and women. These are not a decoration
but the *very core of the Catechism*. In these ardent words
it becomes clear that the doctrine of the faith is spirit
and life. In the middle of the section on "The Church
Is Holy" (CCC 823), there is a well-known text of Saint
Thérèse from the *Autobiographical Writings*, Manuscript B.
In incomparably clear and direct language, it tells us what
the holiness of the Church is:

> If the Church was a body composed of different members,
> it couldn't lack the noblest of all; *it must have a Heart, and
> a Heart BURNING WITH LOVE.* And I realized that *this love
> alone* was the true motive force which enables the other
> members of the Church to act; if it ceased to function, the

Apostles would forget to preach the Gospel, the Martyrs would refuse to shed their blood. LOVE, IN FACT, IS THE VOCATION WHICH INCLUDES ALL OTHERS; IT'S A UNIVERSE OF ITS OWN, COMPRISING ALL TIME AND SPACE—IT'S ETERNAL![6]

Thérèse goes on to say:

Beside myself with joy, I cried out: "Jesus, my love! I've found my vocation, and *my vocation is love.*" I had discovered where it is that I belong in the Church, the niche God has appointed for me. To be nothing else than love, deep down in the heart of Mother Church; that's to be everything at once—my dream wasn't a dream after all![7]

The Council has clearly reminded us that we are *all* called to holiness. But hardly anyone has taught and shown by example as clearly as Saint Thérèse that the way of holiness *really is practicable.* In her "Acte d'offrande à l'Amour miséricordieux" (Act of oblation to Merciful Love) we find words that express with incomparable precision the Catholic doctrine of justification by grace. With these words—they are placed in the Catechism at the end of the chapter on justification, grace, and merit—let us conclude our spiritual exercises. This prayer of Saint Thérèse, this prayer of self-giving, leads us back to where we started and points us forward to the goal for which God created heaven and earth: the Church's home-

---

[6] *Autobiographical Writings*, Manuscript B, 3v; CCC 826.

[7] Ibid.; *The Autobiography of a Saint*, trans. Ronald Knox (London: Harvill Press, 1958), 235.

coming, her return to her heavenly homeland, in the bosom of the Blessed Trinity:

> After earth's exile, I hope to go and enjoy you in the fatherland, but I do not want to lay up merits for heaven. I want to *work for your love alone*. . . . In the evening of this life, I shall appear before you with empty hands, for I do not ask you, Lord, to count my works. All our justice is blemished in your eyes. I wish, then, to be clothed in your own *justice* and to receive from your *love* the eternal possession of *yourself*.[8]

PRAISED BE JESUS CHRIST,
NOW AND FOR EVER! AMEN.

---

[8] "Act of Oblation" in *Story of a Soul*, trans. John Clarke, O.C.D. (Washington, D.C.: Institute of Carmelite Studies, 1981), 277; CCC 2011.